Liz

Lit
on the
Hard shoulder

by the same author

BRILLIANT ADVICE!
MORE BRILLIANT ADVICE!

Life on the Hard Shoulder

by Annie Lawson

A Deirdre McDonald Book
BELLEW PUBLISHING
London

First published in 1990
by Deirdre McDonald Books
Bellew Publishing Co. Ltd.
7 Southampton Place, London WC1A 2DR

Copyright © Annie Lawson 1990

ISBN 0 947792 50 3

Printed in Hong Kong by
Regent Publishing Services Ltd

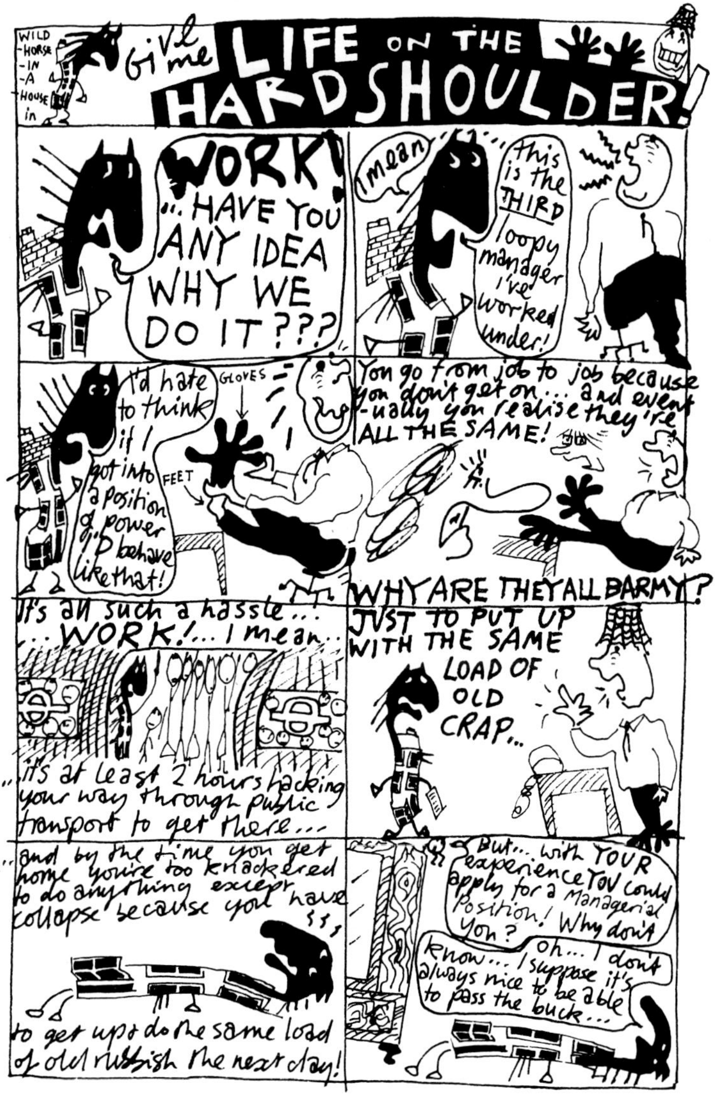
WILD -HORSE -IN -A HOUSE in
Give me LIFE ON THE HARD SHOULDER!
WORK! ... HAVE YOU ANY IDEA WHY WE DO IT???
I mean
this is the THIRD loopy manager I've worked under!
I'd hate to think if I got into a position of power I'D behave like that!
GLOVES
FEET
You go from job to job because you don't get on... and event-ually you realise they're ALL THE SAME!
WHY ARE THEY ALL BARMY?
It's all such a hassle... ...WORK!... I mean...
...it's at least 2 hours hacking your way through public transport to get there...
JUST TO PUT UP WITH THE SAME LOAD OF OLD CRAP...
...and by the time you get home you're too knackered to do anything except collapse because you have
to get up & do the same load of old rubbish the next day!
But... with YOUR experience YOU could apply for a Managerial Position! Why don't you?
Oh... I don't know... I suppose it's always nice to be able to pass the buck...

WET LETTUCE, Pea and MANGO

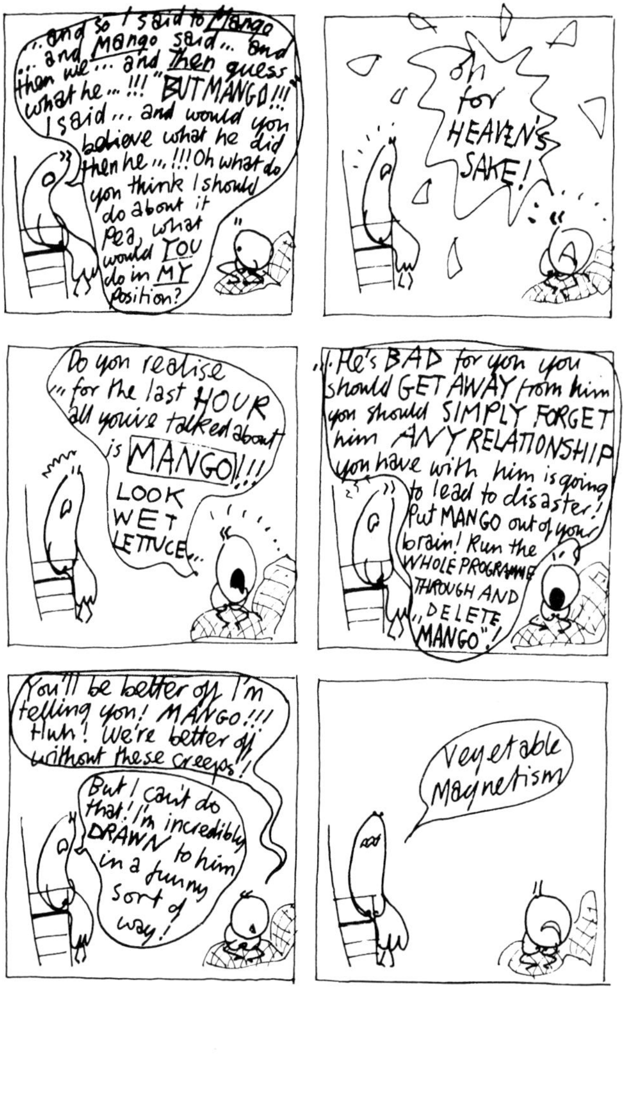
...and so I said to Mango ... and Mango said ... and then we ... and then guess what he ... !!! "BUT MANGO!!!" I said ... and would you believe what he did then he ... !!! Oh what do you think I should do about it Pea, what would YOU do in MY position?"
oh for HEAVEN'S SAKE!
Do you realise ... for the last HOUR all you've talked about is MANGO!!! LOOK WET LETTUCE...
"...He's BAD for you you should GET AWAY from him you should SIMPLY FORGET him ANY RELATIONSHIP you have with him is going to lead to disaster! Put MANGO out of your brain! Run the WHOLE PROGRAMME THROUGH AND "DELETE MANGO"!
You'll be better off I'm telling you! MANGO!!! Huh! We're better off without these creeps!
But I can't do that! I'm incredibly DRAWN to him in a funny sort of way!
Vegetable Magnetism

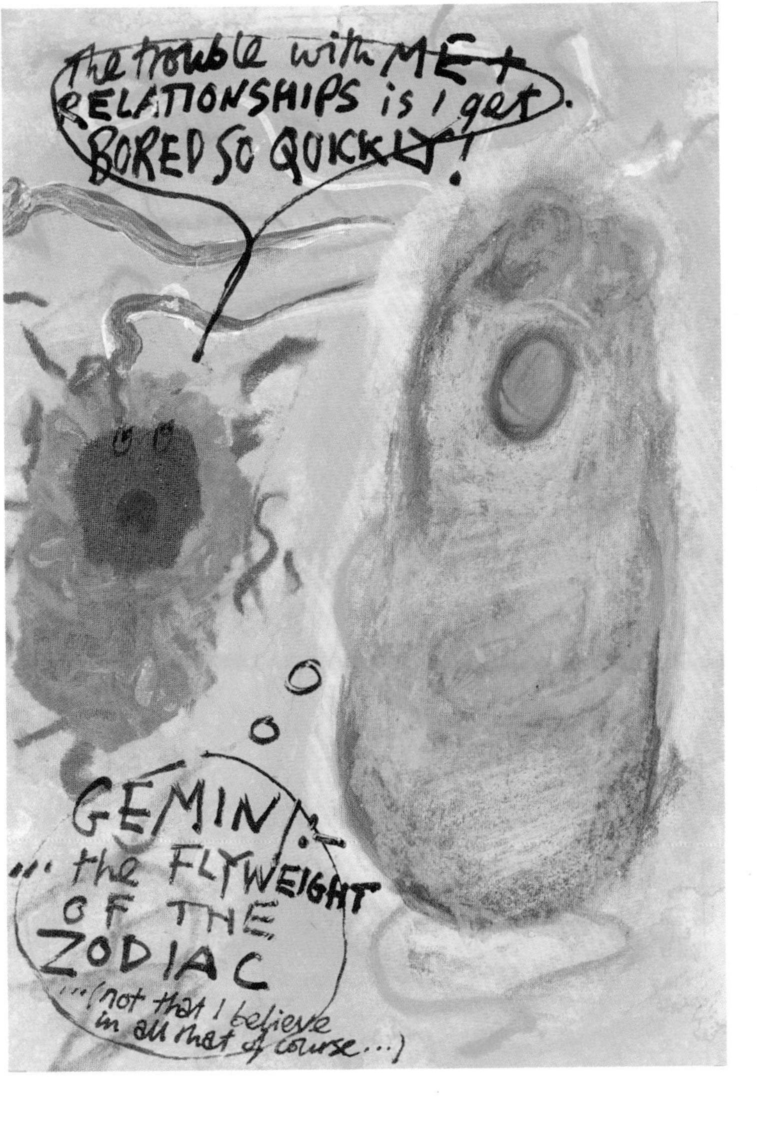

The trouble with ME + RELATIONSHIPS is I get BORED SO QUICKLY!
GEMINI: .. the FLYWEIGHT OF THE ZODIAC
... (not that I believe in all that of course...)

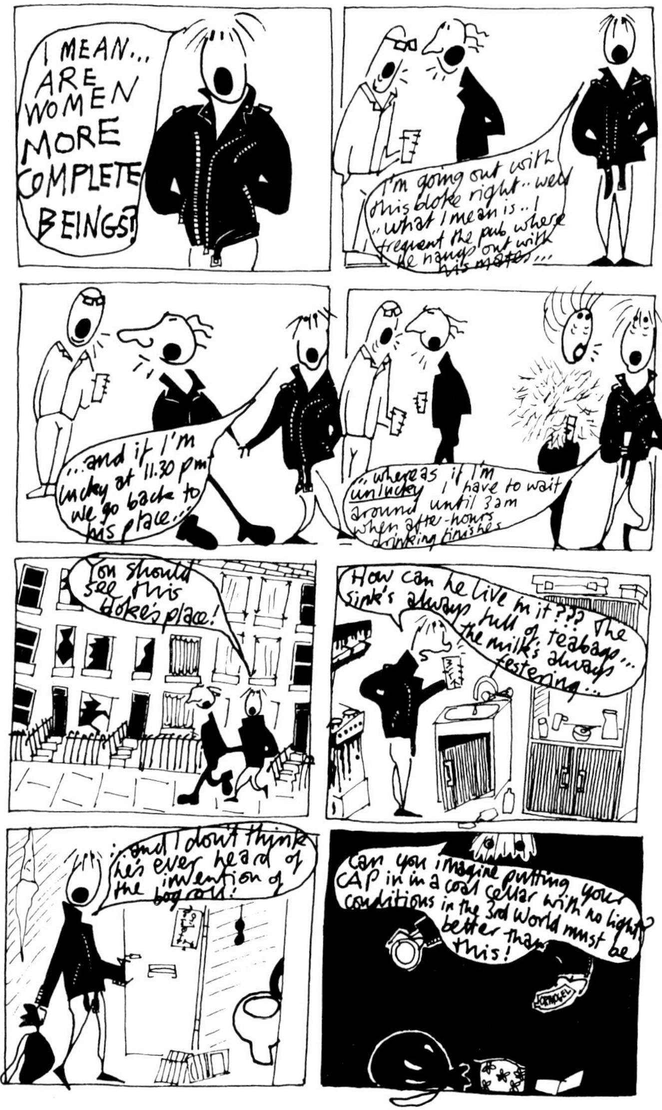
I MEAN... ARE WOMEN MORE COMPLETE BEINGS?
I'm going out with this bloke right.. well ..what I mean is.. I frequent the pub where he hangs out with his mates...
...and if I'm lucky at 11.30 pm we go back to his place...
...whereas if I'm unlucky I have to wait around until 3am when after-hours drinking finishes
You should see this bloke's place!
How can he live in it??? The sink's always full of teabags... the milk's always festering...
...and I don't think he's ever heard of the invention of the bog roll!
Can you imagine putting your CAP in in a coal cellar with no light? conditions in the 3rd World must be better than this!

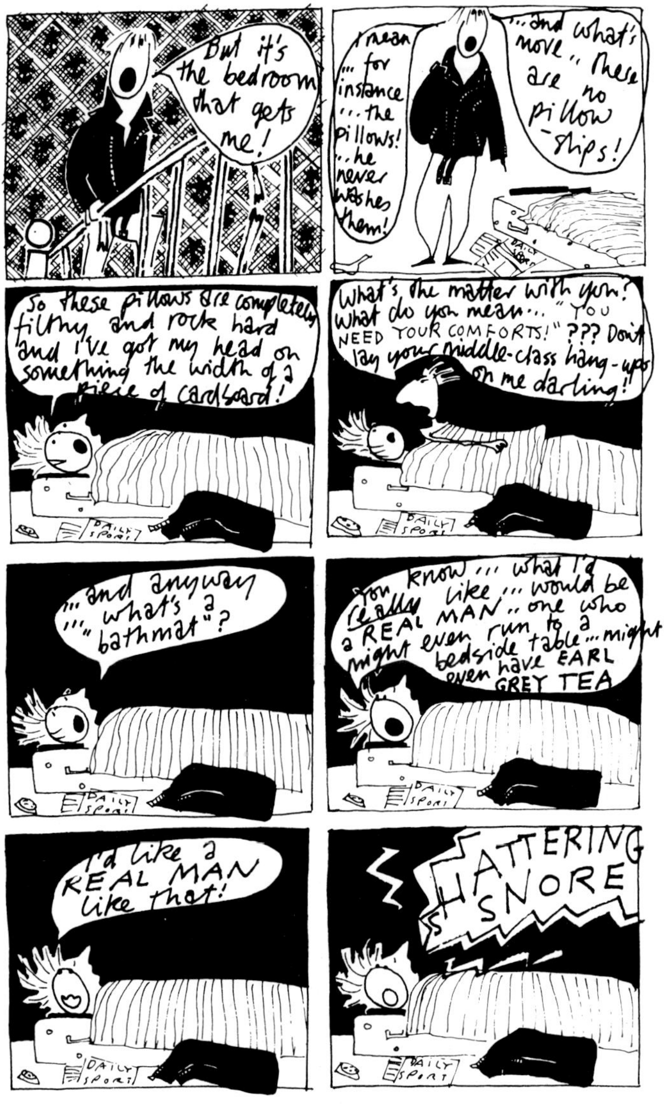
But it's the bedroom that gets me!
I mean ... for instance ... the pillows! ... he never washes them!
... and what's more ... there are no pillow-slips!
DAILY SPORT
So these pillows are completely filthy and rock hard and I've got my head on something the width of a piece of cardboard!
DAILY SPORT
What's the matter with you? What do you mean ... "YOU NEED YOUR COMFORTS!" ??? Don't lay your middle-class hang-ups on me darling!
DAILY SPORT
... and anyway ... what's a ... "bathmat"?
DAILY SPORT
You know ... what I'd really like ... would be a REAL MAN ... one who might even run to a bedside table ... might even have EARL GREY TEA
DAILY SPORT
I'd like a REAL MAN like that!
DAILY SPORT
SHATTERING SNORE
DAILY SPORT

WETLETTUCE Still can't stop

... and anyway ... a MANGO's a FRUIT! I'm certain a mango's a FRUIT not a veg! You're hung up on a FRUIT!
CAN'T STOP THINKING ABOUT MANGO
WET LETTUCE
PEA
Whoever heard of anything so stupid!!! A LETTUCE and a MANGO! It'll never work! What a bloody weird combination THAT is!
I don't see why not!
Why not? Don't be fruit-ist!
ANYWAY... You want to FORGET about him & go out and meet someone more progressive!.. someone who can TALK about their FEELINGS + KNOWS HOW TO RELATE! Someone who...
... is cognizant of political issues and who CARES ABOUT THE ENVIRON-MENT! You need some SWITCHED-ON VEG! ... some AWARE VEG... some NEW-AGE VEG!
You mean some boring old ex-braindead hippy GREEN VEG? Thanks very much! I don't have trouble sleeping thank-you!
No! NO! You need someone with a bit more spunk! I know what you want!
I want a certain degree of excitement but not so much that I go mad...
I know what would be just right for you!
... A NEW POTATO!

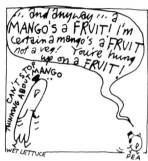

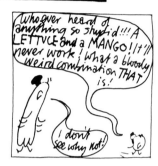

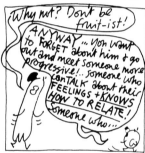

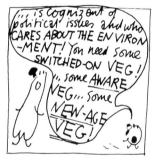

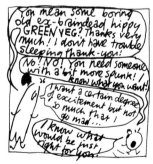

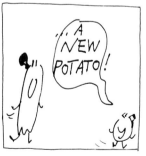

Thinking about MANGO

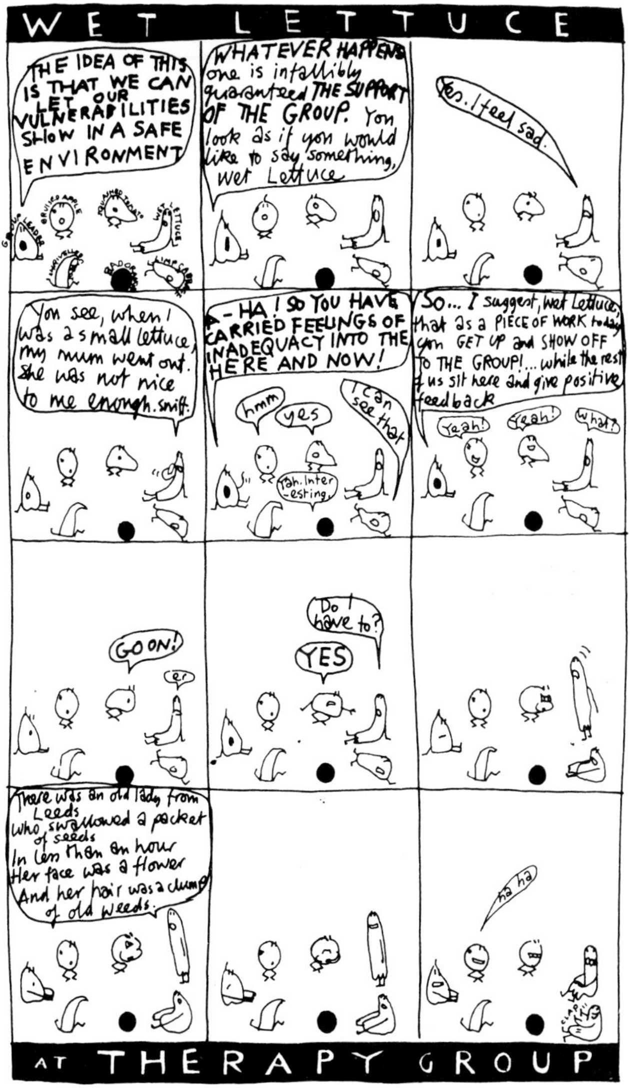
WET LETTUCE
THE IDEA OF THIS IS THAT WE CAN LET OUR VULNERABILITIES SHOW IN A SAFE ENVIRONMENT
GROUP LEADER
BRUISED APPLE
SQUASHED TOMATO
WET LETTUCE
WHATEVER HAPPENS one is infallibly guaranteed THE SUPPORT OF THE GROUP. You look as if you would like to say something, Wet Lettuce
Yes. I feel sad.
You see, when I was a small lettuce, my mum went out. She was not nice to me enough. sniff.
A-HA! SO YOU HAVE CARRIED FEELINGS OF INADEQUACY INTO THE HERE AND NOW!
hmm
yes
I can see that
Yeah. Interesting.
So... I suggest, Wet Lettuce, that as a PIECE OF WORK today you GET UP and SHOW OFF TO THE GROUP!... while the rest of us sit here and give positive feedback
Yeah!
Yeah!
what?
GO ON!
er
Do I have to?
YES
There was an old lady from Leeds
Who swallowed a packet of seeds
In less than an hour
Her face was a flower
And her hair was a clump of old weeds.
ha ha
AT THERAPY GROUP

The Gas Bill

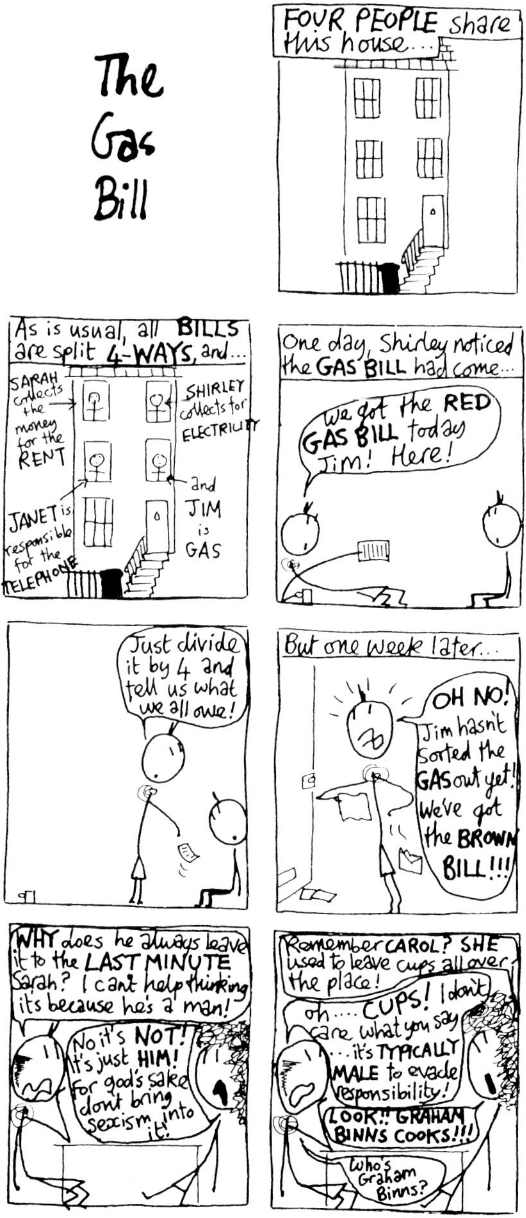

FOUR PEOPLE share this house...
As is usual, all BILLS are split 4-WAYS, and...
SARAH collects the money for the RENT
SHIRLEY collects for ELECTRICITY
JANET is responsible for the TELEPHONE
and JIM is GAS
One day, Shirley noticed the GAS BILL had come...
We got the RED GAS BILL today Jim! Here!
Just divide it by 4 and tell us what we all owe!
But one week later...
OH NO! Jim hasn't sorted the GAS out yet! We've got the BROWN BILL!!!
WHY does he always leave it to the LAST MINUTE Sarah? I can't help thinking it's because he's a man!
No it's NOT! it's just HIM! for god's sake don't bring sexism into it!
Remember CAROL? SHE used to leave cups all over the place!
oh.... CUPS! I don't care what you say ... it's TYPICALLY MALE to evade responsibility!
LOOK!! GRAHAM BINNS COOKS!!!
Who's Graham Binns?

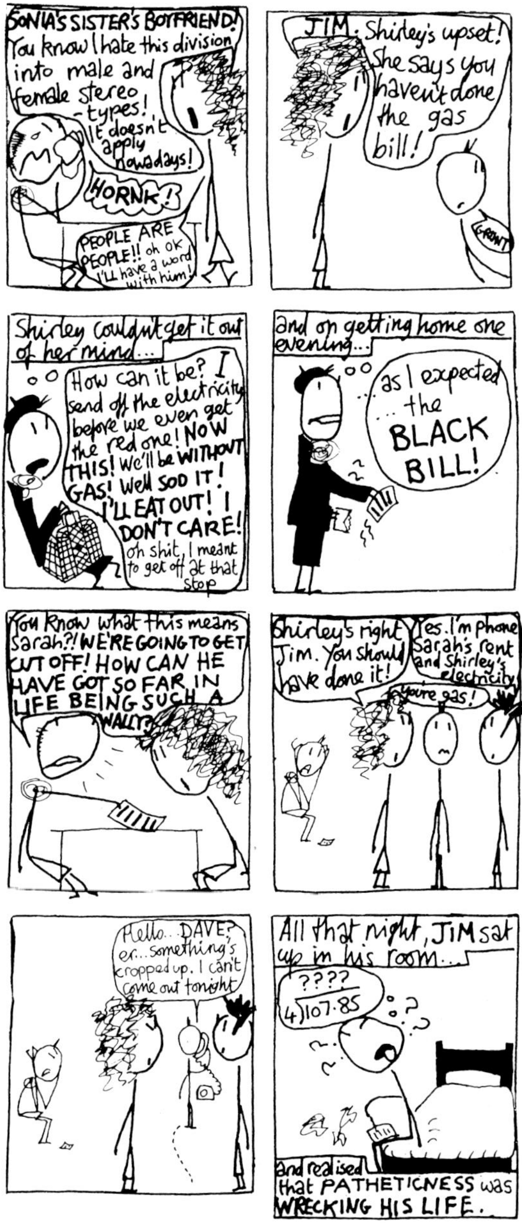
SONIA'S SISTER'S BOYFRIEND! You know I hate this division into male and female stereo-types! It doesn't apply nowadays!
HORNK!
PEOPLE ARE PEOPLE!! oh OK I'LL have a word with him!
JIM: Shirley's upset! She says you haven't done the gas bill!
GRONT
Shirley couldn't get it out of her mind...
How can it be? I send off the electricity before we even get the red one! NOW THIS! We'll be WITHOUT GAS! Well SOD IT! I'LL EAT OUT! I DON'T CARE!
oh shit, I meant to get off at that stop
and on getting home one evening...
...as I expected ...the BLACK BILL!
You know what this means Sarah?! WE'RE GOING TO GET CUT OFF! HOW CAN HE HAVE GOT SO FAR IN LIFE BEING SUCH A WALLY?!
Shirley's right Jim. You should have done it!
Yes. I'm phone Sarah's rent and Shirley's electricity
You're gas!
Hello... DAVE? er... something's cropped up. I can't come out tonight
All that night, JIM sat up in his room...
????
4)107.85
and realised that PATHETICNESS was WRECKING HIS LIFE.

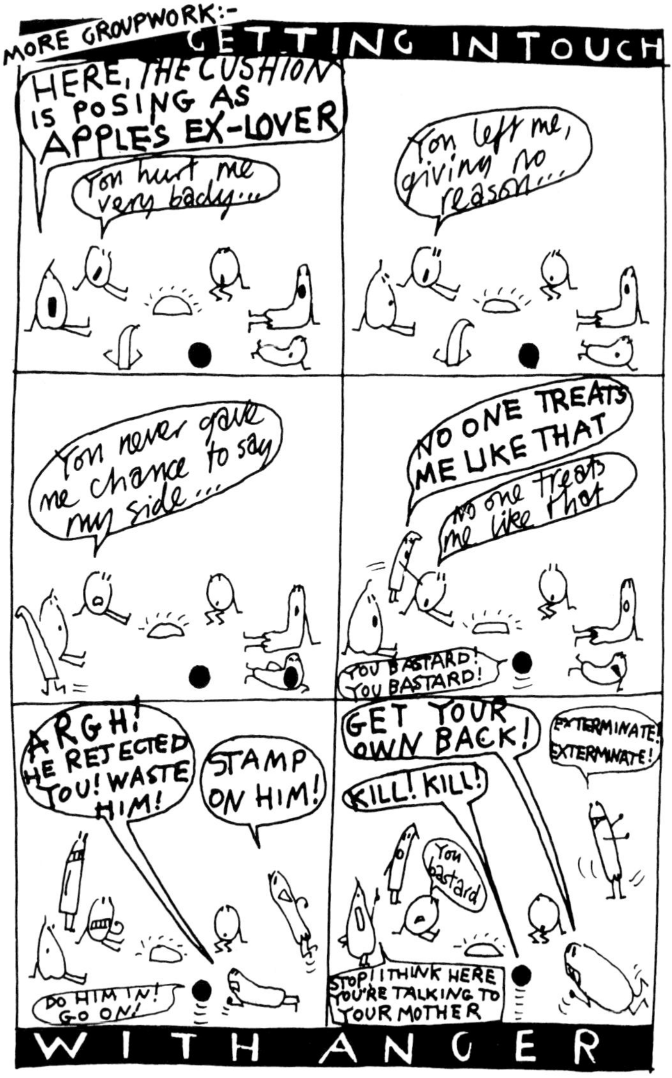
MORE GROUPWORK:- GETTING INTOUCH
HERE, THE CUSHION IS POSING AS APPLE'S EX-LOVER
You hurt me very badly...
You left me, giving no reason...
You never gave me chance to say my side...
NO ONE TREATS ME LIKE THAT
No one treats me like that
YOU BASTARD! YOU BASTARD!
ARGH! HE REJECTED YOU! WASTE HIM!
STAMP ON HIM!
DO HIM IN! GO ON!
GET YOUR OWN BACK!
EXTERMINATE! EXTERMINATE!
KILL! KILL!
You bastard
STOP! I THINK HERE YOU'RE TALKING TO YOUR MOTHER
WITH ANGER

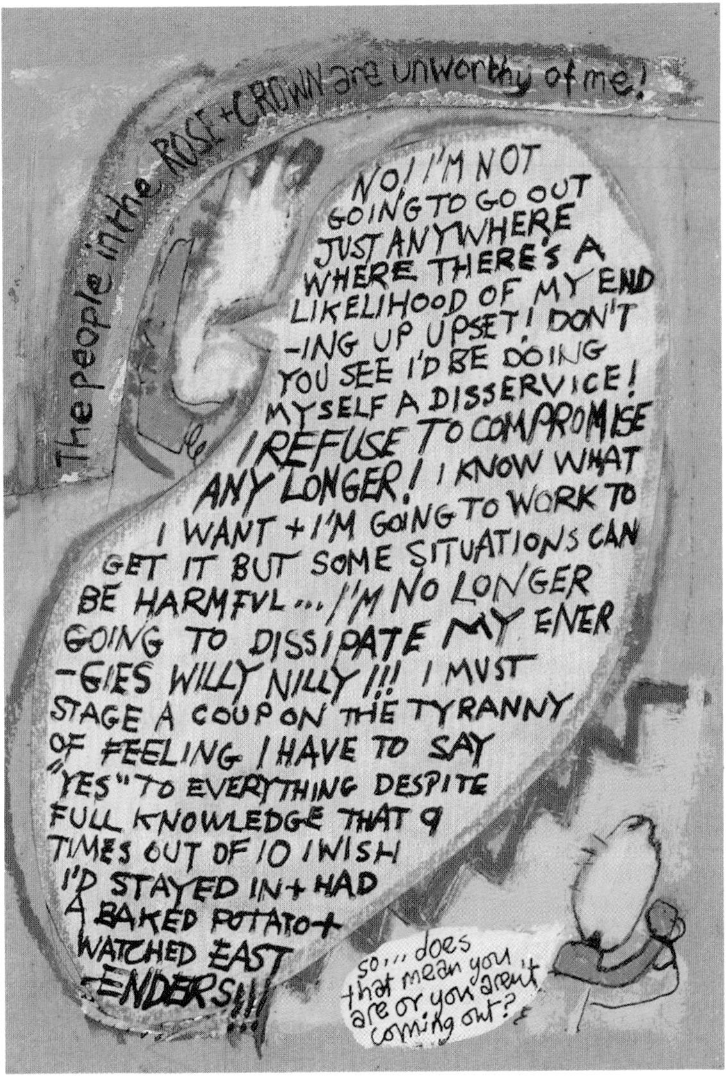

The people in the ROSE + CROWN are unworthy of me!
NO! I'M NOT GOING TO GO OUT JUST ANYWHERE WHERE THERE'S A LIKELIHOOD OF MY END -ING UP UPSET! DON'T YOU SEE I'D BE DOING MYSELF A DISSERVICE! I REFUSE TO COMPROMISE ANY LONGER! I KNOW WHAT I WANT + I'M GOING TO WORK TO GET IT BUT SOME SITUATIONS CAN BE HARMFUL... I'M NO LONGER GOING TO DISSIPATE MY ENER -GIES WILLY NILLY!!! I MUST STAGE A COUP ON THE TYRANNY OF FEELING I HAVE TO SAY "YES" TO EVERYTHING DESPITE FULL KNOWLEDGE THAT 9 TIMES OUT OF 10 I WISH I'D STAYED IN + HAD A BAKED POTATO + WATCHED EAST ENDERS!!!
so... does that mean you are or you aren't coming out?

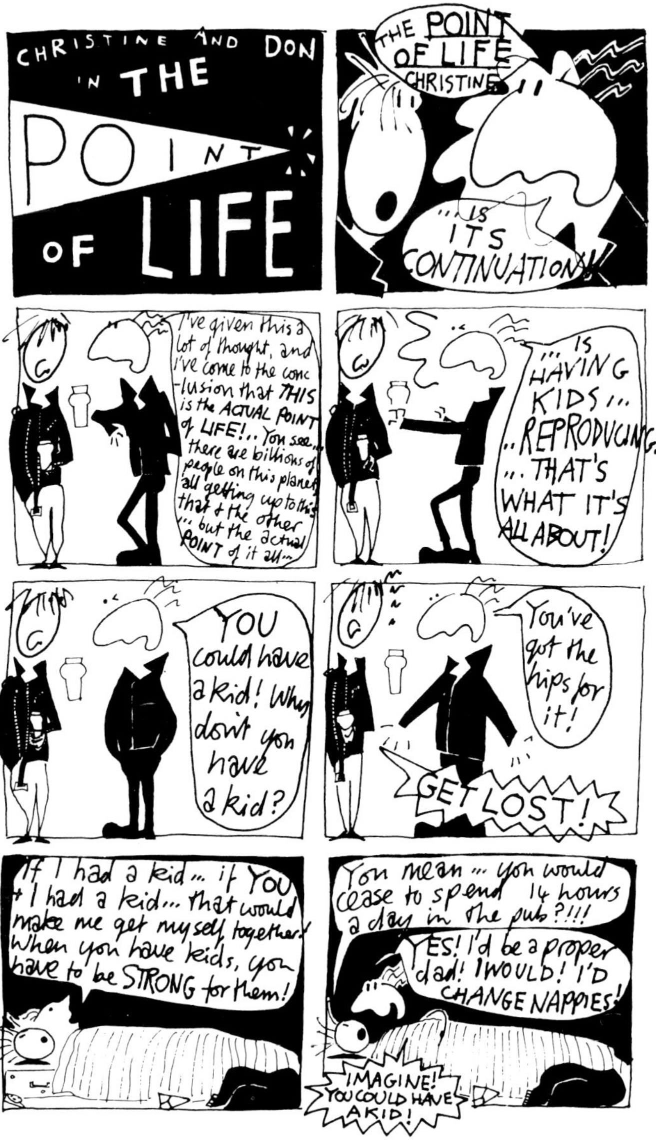
CHRISTINE AND DON IN THE POINT OF LIFE
THE POINT OF LIFE CHRISTINE
...IS ITS CONTINUATION!
I've given this a lot of thought, and I've come to the conclusion that THIS is the ACTUAL POINT of LIFE!.. You see.. there are billions of people on this planet all getting up to this that & the other .. but the actual POINT of it all...
... IS HAVING KIDS... ..REPRODUCING! ... THAT'S WHAT IT'S ALL ABOUT!
YOU could have a kid! Why don't you have a kid?
You've got the hips for it!
GET LOST!
If I had a kid... if YOU + I had a kid... that would make me get myself together! When you have kids, you have to be STRONG for them!
You mean... you would cease to spend 14 hours a day in the pub?!!!
YES! I'd be a proper dad! I WOULD! I'D CHANGE NAPPIES!
IMAGINE! YOU COULD HAVE A KID!

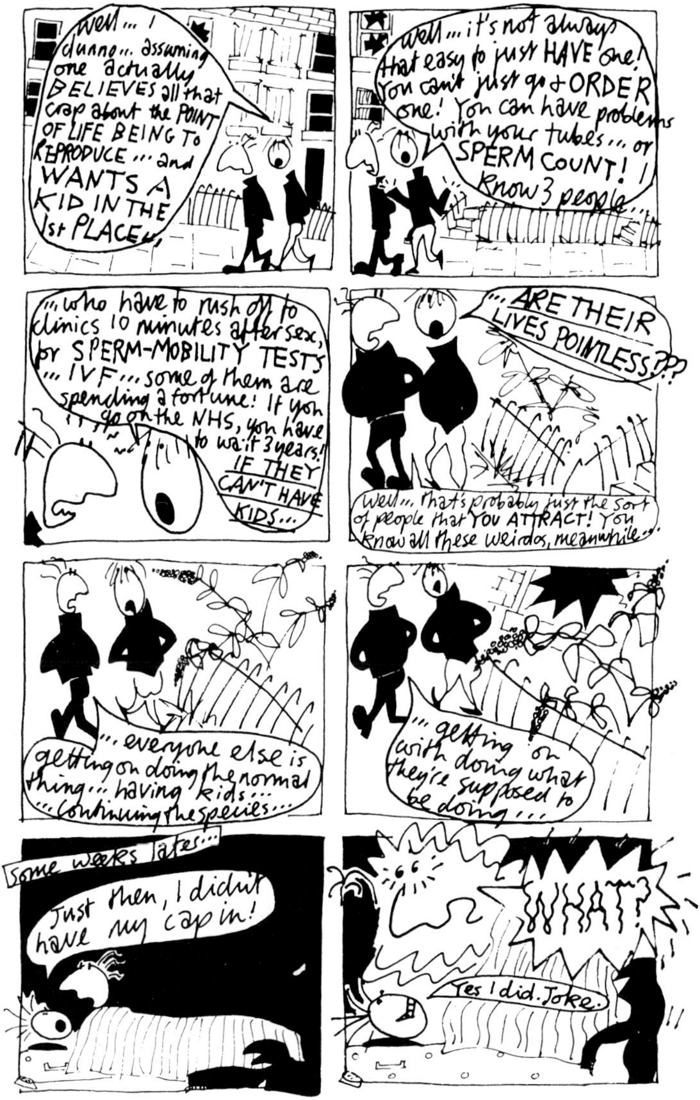
Well... I dunno... assuming one actually BELIEVES all that crap about the POINT OF LIFE BEING TO REPRODUCE... and WANTS A KID IN THE 1st PLACE...
Well... it's not always that easy to just HAVE one! You can't just go & ORDER one! You can have problems with your tubes... or SPERM COUNT! I know 3 people...
...who have to rush off to clinics 10 minutes after sex, or SPERM-MOBILITY TESTS... IVF... some of them are spending a fortune! If you go on the NHS, you have to wait 3 years! IF THEY CAN'T HAVE KIDS...
...ARE THEIR LIVES POINTLESS???
Well... that's probably just the sort of people that YOU ATTRACT! You know all these weirdos, meanwhile...
...everyone else is getting on doing the normal thing... having kids... ...continuing the species...
...getting on with doing what they're supposed to be doing...
Some weeks later...
Just then, I didn't have my cap in!
WHAT?
Yes I did. Joke.

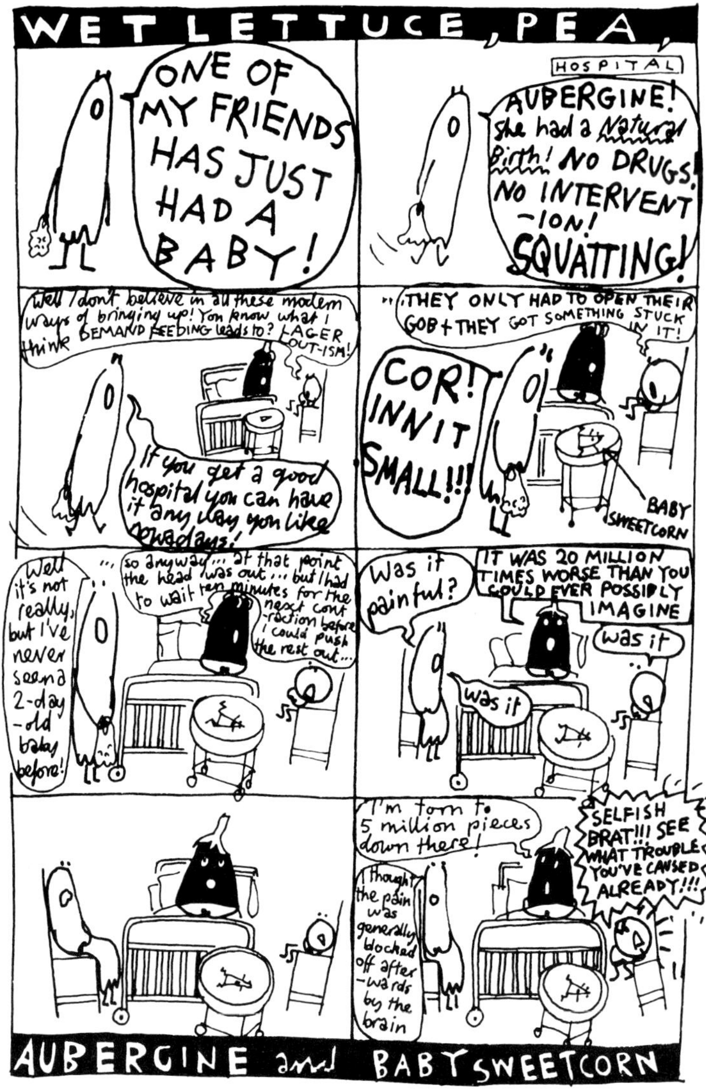
WET LETTUCE, PEA,
ONE OF MY FRIENDS HAS JUST HAD A BABY!
HOSPITAL
AUBERGINE! She had a Natural Birth! NO DRUGS! NO INTERVENT-ION! SQUATTING!
Well I don't believe in all these modern ways of bringing up! You know what I think DEMAND FEEDING leads to? LAGER LOUT-ISM!
If you get a good hospital you can have it any way you like nowadays!
...THEY ONLY HAD TO OPEN THEIR GOB + THEY GOT SOMETHING STUCK IN IT!
COR! INNIT SMALL!!!
BABY SWEETCORN
Well it's not really, but I've never seen a 2-day-old baby before!
... so anyway... at that point the head was out... but I had to wait ten minutes for the next cont-raction before I could push the rest out...
Was it painful?
IT WAS 20 MILLION TIMES WORSE THAN YOU COULD EVER POSSIBLY IMAGINE
was it
was it
I'm torn to 5 million pieces down there!
I thought the pain was generally blocked off after-wards by the brain
SELFISH BRAT!!! SEE WHAT TROUBLE YOU'VE CAUSED ALREADY!!!
AUBERGINE and BABY SWEETCORN

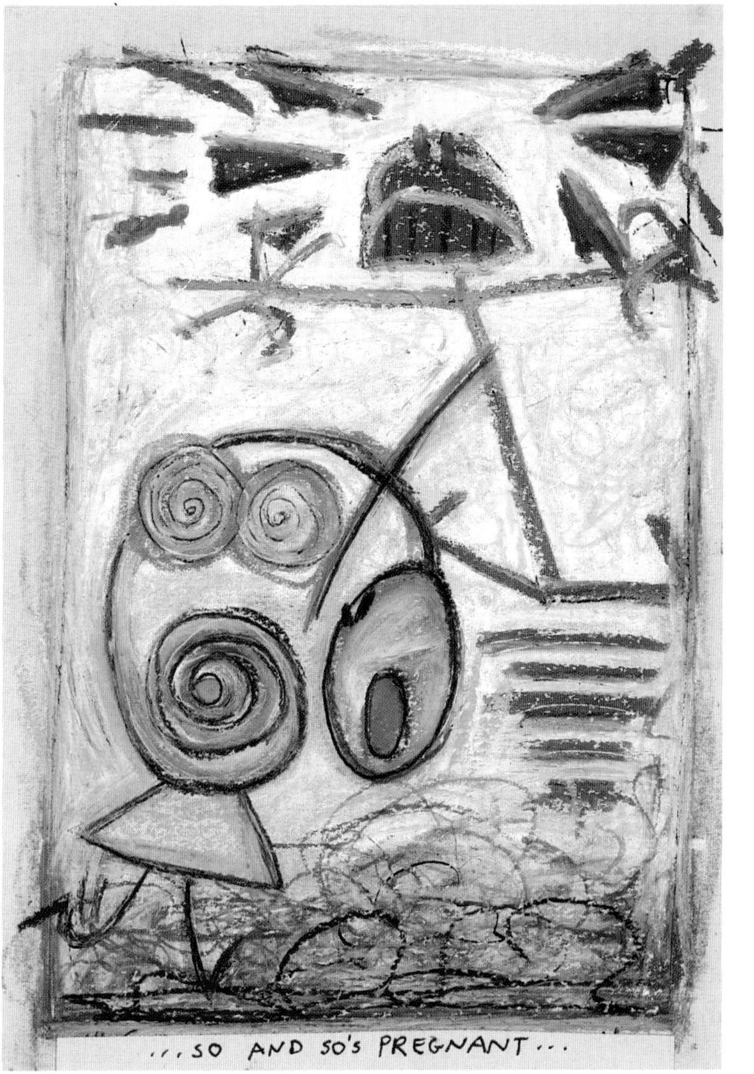

...SO AND SO's PREGNANT...

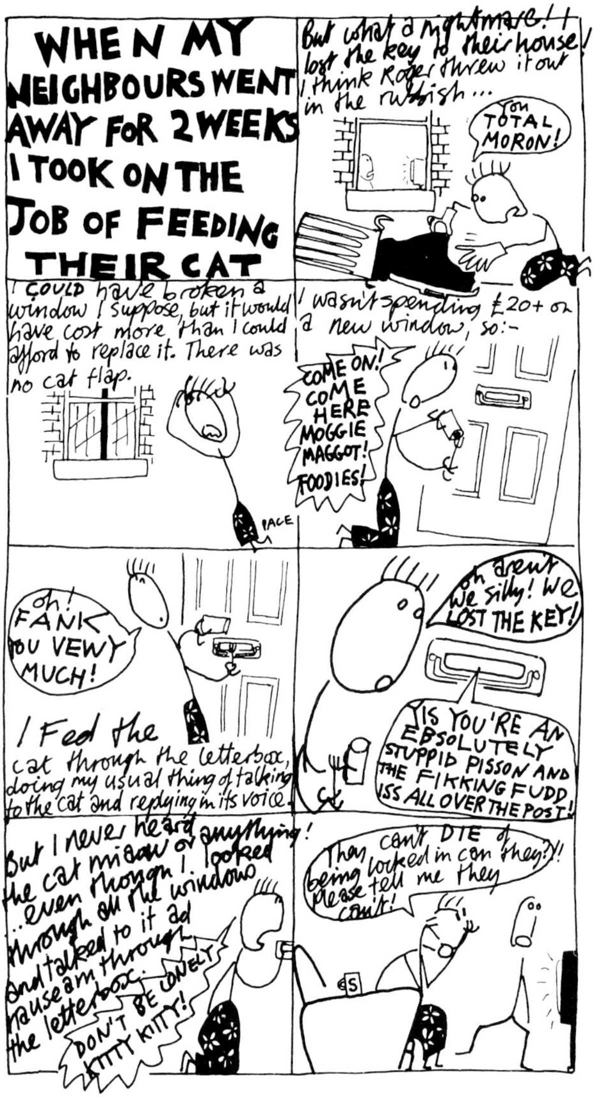
WHEN MY NEIGHBOURS WENT AWAY FOR 2 WEEKS I TOOK ON THE JOB OF FEEDING THEIR CAT
But what a nightmare! I lost the key to their house! I think Roger threw it out in the rubbish...
You TOTAL MORON!
I COULD have broken a window I suppose, but it would have cost more than I could afford to replace it. There was no cat flap.
PACE
I wasn't spending £20+ on a new window, so:-
COME ON! COME HERE MOGGIE MAGGOT! FOODIES!
Oh! FANK YOU VEWY MUCH!
I Fed the cat through the letterbox, doing my usual thing of talking to the cat and replying in its voice.
Oh aren't we silly! We LOST THE KEY!
IS YOU'RE AN EBSOLUTELY STUPPID PISSON AND THE FIKKING FUDD ISS ALL OVER THE POST!
But I never heard the cat miaow or anything! ...even though I looked through all the windows and talked to it ad nauseam through the letterbox.
DON'T BE LONELY KITTY KITTY!
They can't DIE of being locked in can they?!! Please tell me they can't!

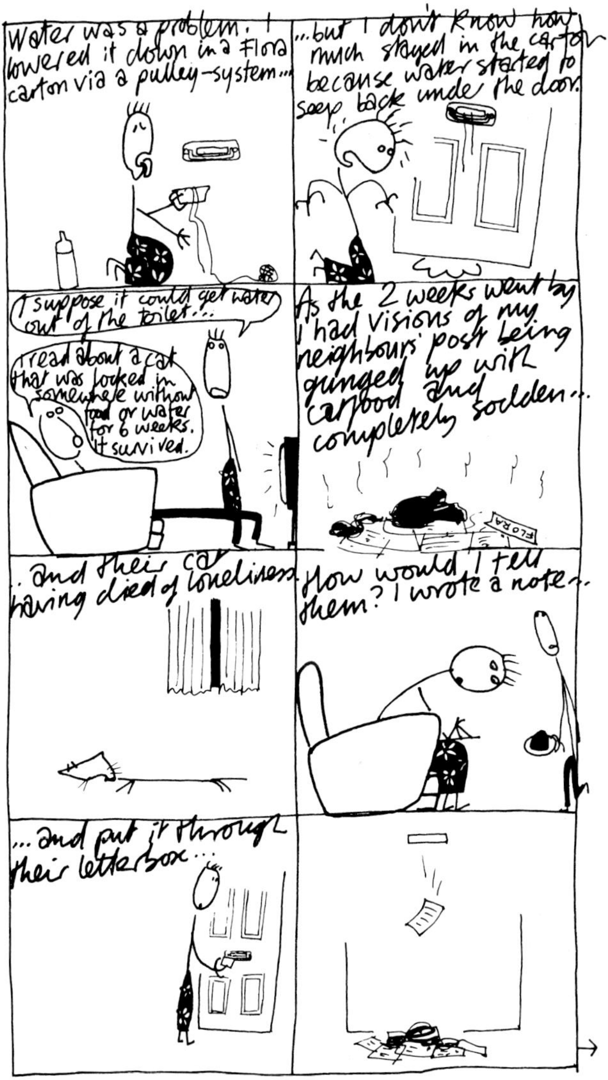
Water was a problem. I lowered it down in a Flora carton via a pulley-system...
...but I don't know how much stayed in the carton because water started to seep back under the door.
I suppose it could get water out of the toilet...
I read about a cat that was locked in somewhere without food or water for 6 weeks. It survived.
As the 2 weeks went by I had visions of my neighbours' post being gunged up with catfood and completely sodden...
FLORA
...and their cat having died of loneliness.
How would I tell them? I wrote a note...
...and put it through their letterbox...

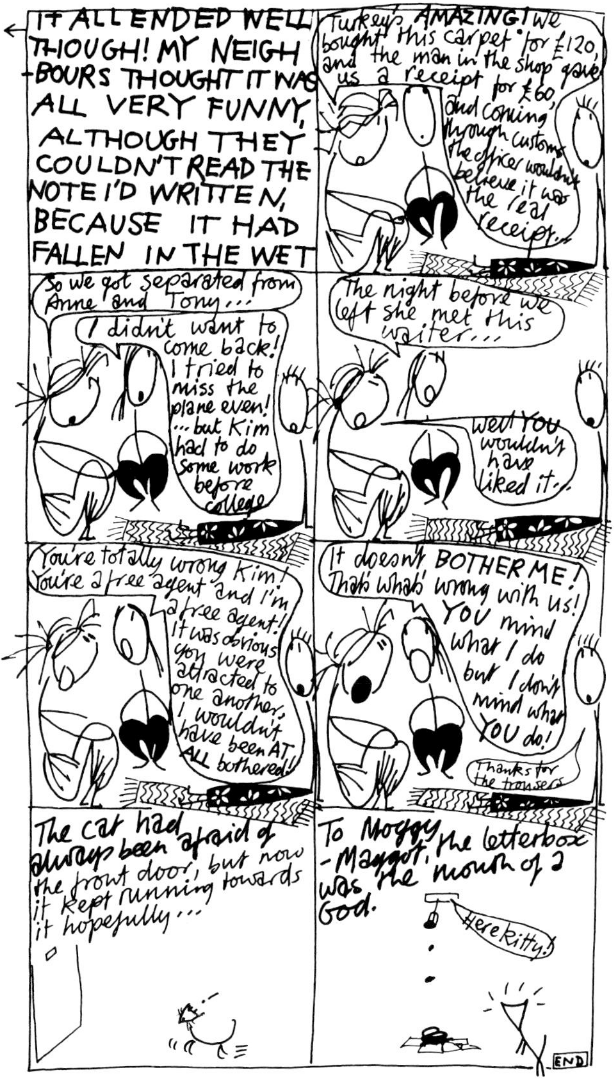
IT ALL ENDED WELL THOUGH! MY NEIGHBOURS THOUGHT IT WAS ALL VERY FUNNY, ALTHOUGH THEY COULDN'T READ THE NOTE I'D WRITTEN, BECAUSE IT HAD FALLEN IN THE WET
Turkey's AMAZING! We bought this carpet for £120, and the man in the shop gave us a receipt for £60, and coming through customs the officer wouldn't believe it was the real receipt...
So we got separated from Anne and Tony...
I didn't want to come back! I tried to miss the plane even! ...but Kim had to do some work before college
The night before we left she met this waiter...
Well YOU wouldn't have liked it...
You're totally wrong Kim! You're a free agent and I'm a free agent! It was obvious you were attracted to one another, I wouldn't have been AT ALL bothered!
It doesn't BOTHER ME! That's what's wrong with us! YOU mind what I do but I don't mind what YOU do!
Thanks for the trousers
The cat had always been afraid of the front door, but now it kept running towards it hopefully...
To Moggy-Maggot, the letterbox was the mouth of a God.
Here Kitty!
END

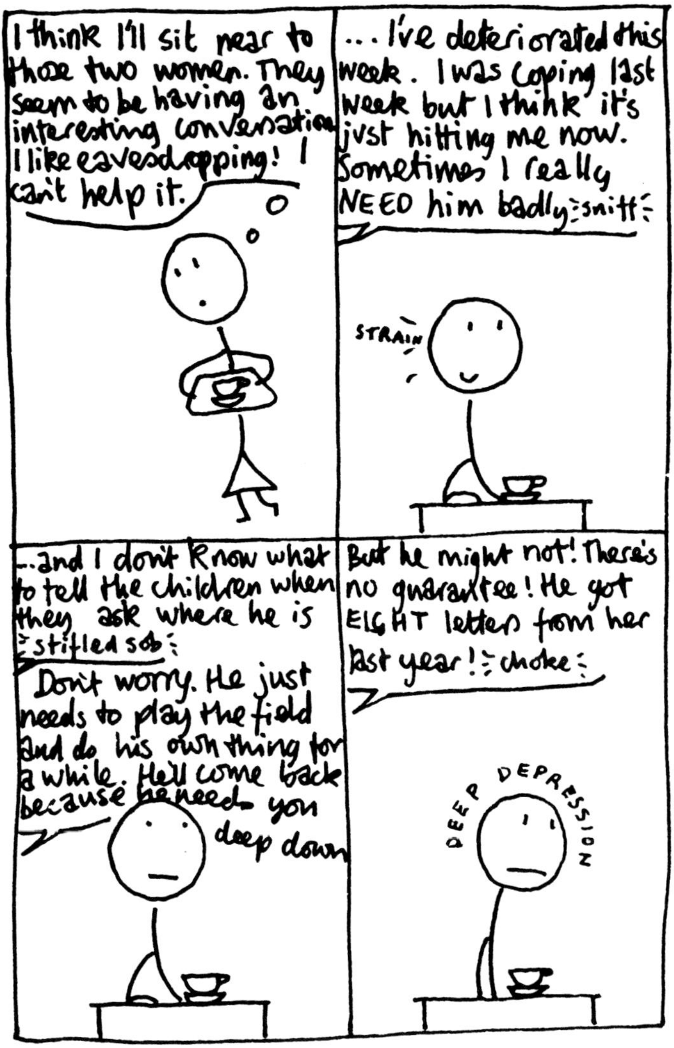
I think I'll sit near to those two women. They seem to be having an interesting conversation. I like eavesdropping! I can't help it.
... I've deteriorated this week. I was coping last week but I think it's just hitting me now. Sometimes I really NEED him badly ≈sniff≈
STRAIN
...and I don't know what to tell the children when they ask where he is ≈stifled sob≈
Don't worry. He just needs to play the field and do his own thing for a while. He'll come back because he needs you deep down
But he might not! There's no guarantee! He got EIGHT letters from her last year! ≈choke≈
DEEP DEPRESSION

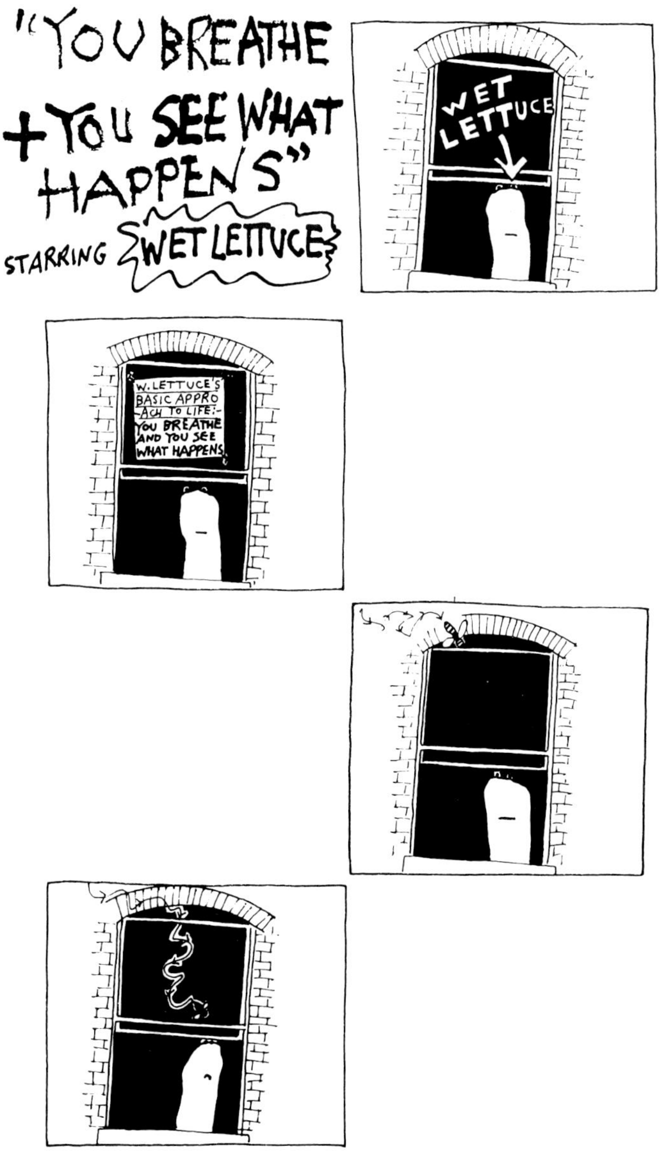
"YOU BREATHE + YOU SEE WHAT HAPPENS"
STARRING WET LETTUCE
WET LETTUCE
W. LETTUCE'S BASIC APPRO-ACH TO LIFE:-
YOU BREATHE AND YOU SEE WHAT HAPPENS

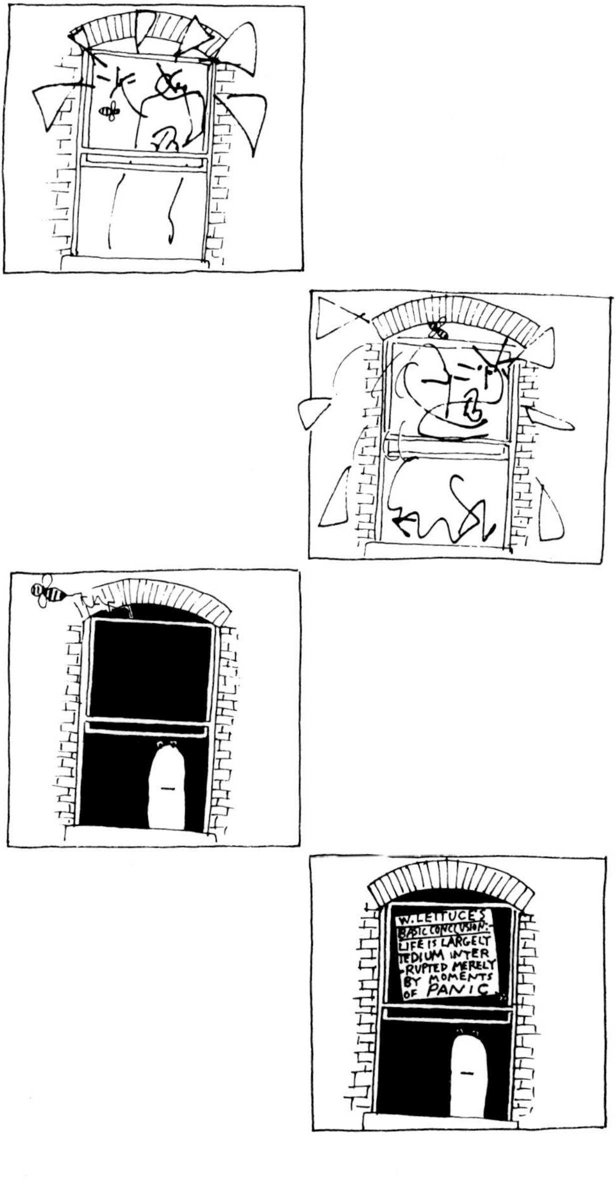
W. LETTUCE'S
BASIC CONCLUSION:-
LIFE IS LARGELY TEDIUM INTER-RUPTED MERELY BY MOMENTS OF PANIC.

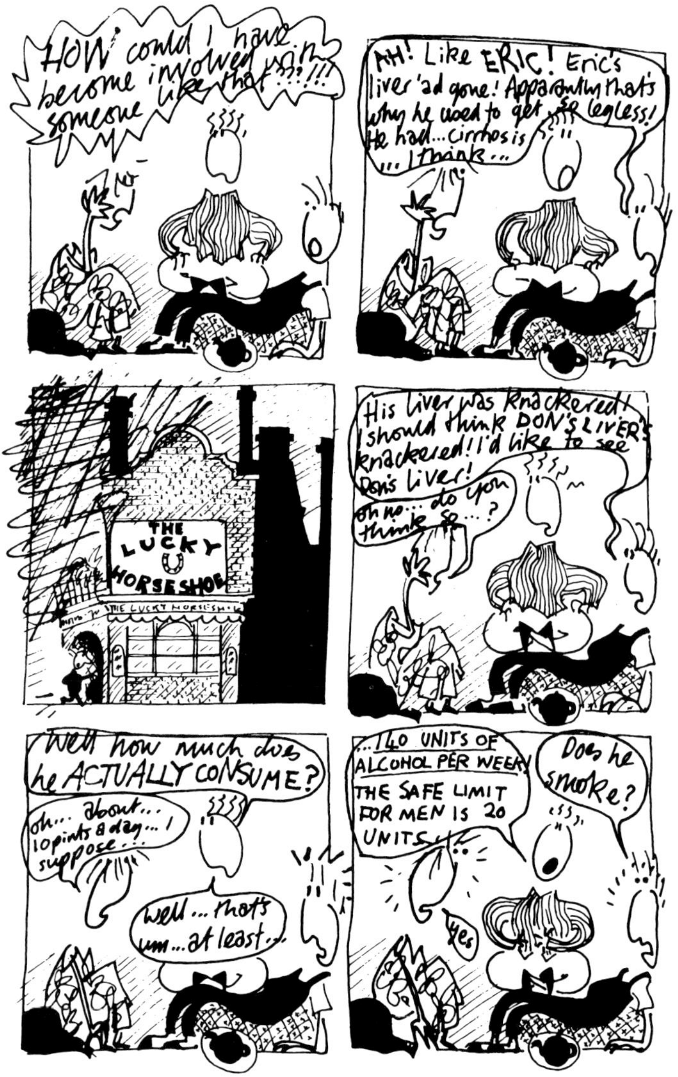
HOW could I have become involved with someone like that???!!!
AH! Like ERIC! Eric's liver 'ad gone! Apparently that's why he used to get so legless! He had... cirrhosis is ... I think...
THE LUCKY HORSESHOE
His liver was knackered! I should think DON'S LIVER'S knackered! I'd like to see Don's liver!
oh no... do you think so...?
Well how much does he ACTUALLY CONSUME?
oh... about... 10 pints a day... I suppose...
well... that's um... at least...
...140 UNITS OF ALCOHOL PER WEEK! THE SAFE LIMIT FOR MEN IS 20 UNITS.
Does he smoke?
Yes

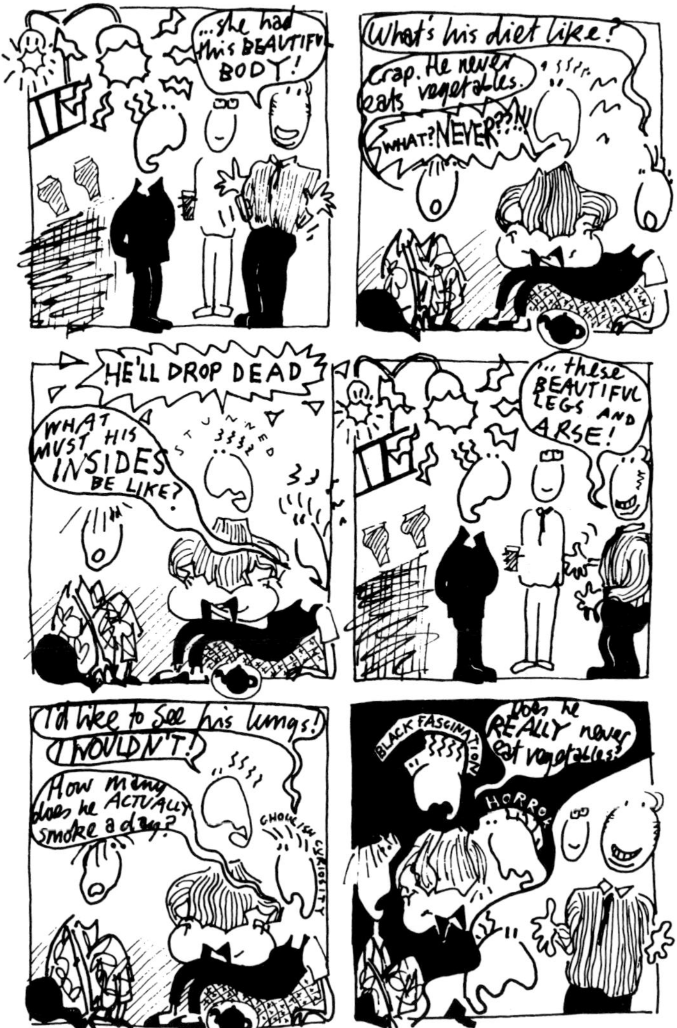
...she had this BEAUTIFUL BODY!
What's his diet like?
Crap. He never eats vegetables.
WHAT? NEVER??!!
HE'LL DROP DEAD
WHAT MUST HIS INSIDES BE LIKE?
STUNNED
...these BEAUTIFUL LEGS AND ARSE!
I'd like to see his lungs!
I WOULDN'T!
How many does he ACTUALLY smoke a day?
GHOULISH CURIOSITY
BLACK FASCINATION
Does he REALLY never eat vegetables?
HORROR

Phallocracy fails the Female!

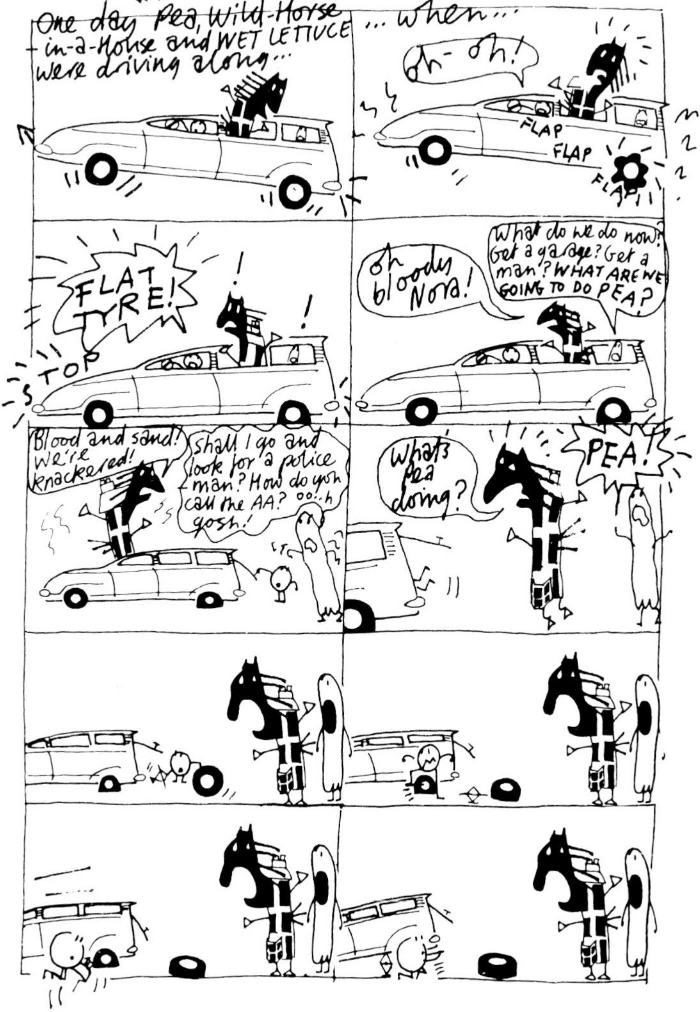
One day Pea, Wild-Horse-in-a-Horse and WET LETTUCE were driving along...
... when...
Oh-oh!
FLAP
FLAP
FLAP
FLAT TYRE!
STOP
Oh bloody Nora!
What do we do now? Get a garage? Get a man? WHAT ARE WE GOING TO DO PEA?
Blood and sand! We're knackered!
Shall I go and look for a police man? How do you call the AA? oo..h gosh!
What's Pea doing?
PEA!

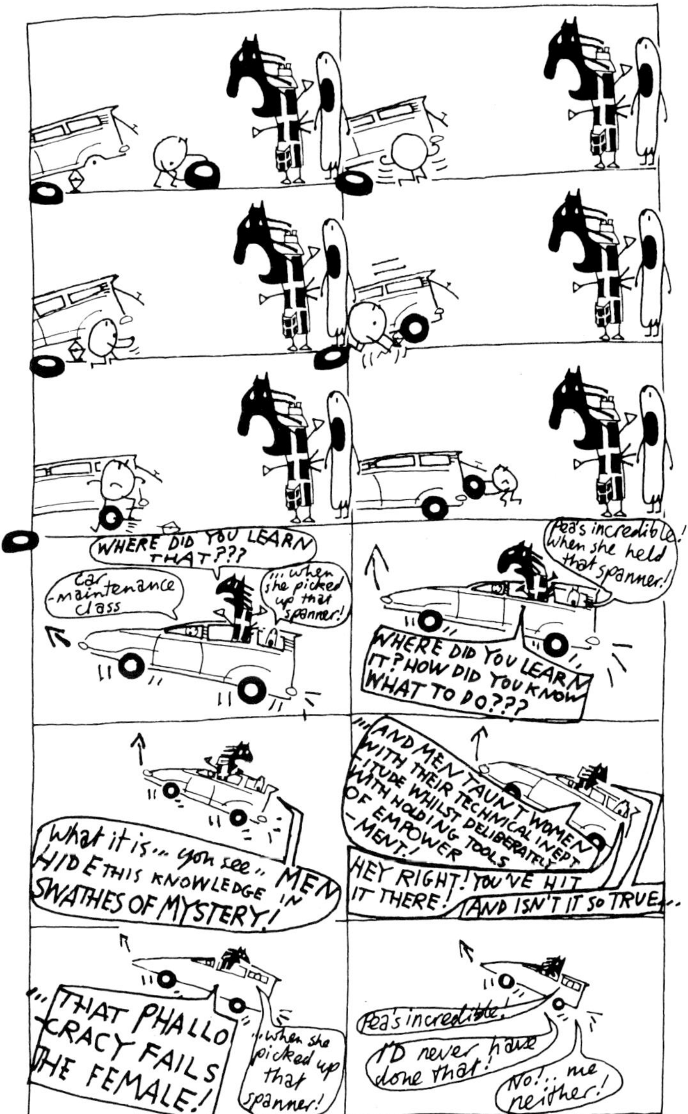

WHERE DID YOU LEARN THAT???
Car-maintenance class
...when she picked up that spanner!
Pea's incredible! When she held that spanner!
WHERE DID YOU LEARN IT? HOW DID YOU KNOW WHAT TO DO???
What it is... you see... MEN HIDE THIS KNOWLEDGE IN SWATHES OF MYSTERY!
...AND MEN TAUNT WOMEN WITH THEIR TECHNICAL INEPT-ITUDE WHILST DELIBERATELY WITHHOLDING TOOLS OF EMPOWER-MENT!
HEY RIGHT! YOU'VE HIT IT THERE!
AND ISN'T IT SO TRUE...
...THAT PHALLOCRACY FAILS THE FEMALE!
...when she picked up that spanner!
Pea's incredible!
I'D never have done that!
No!.. me neither!

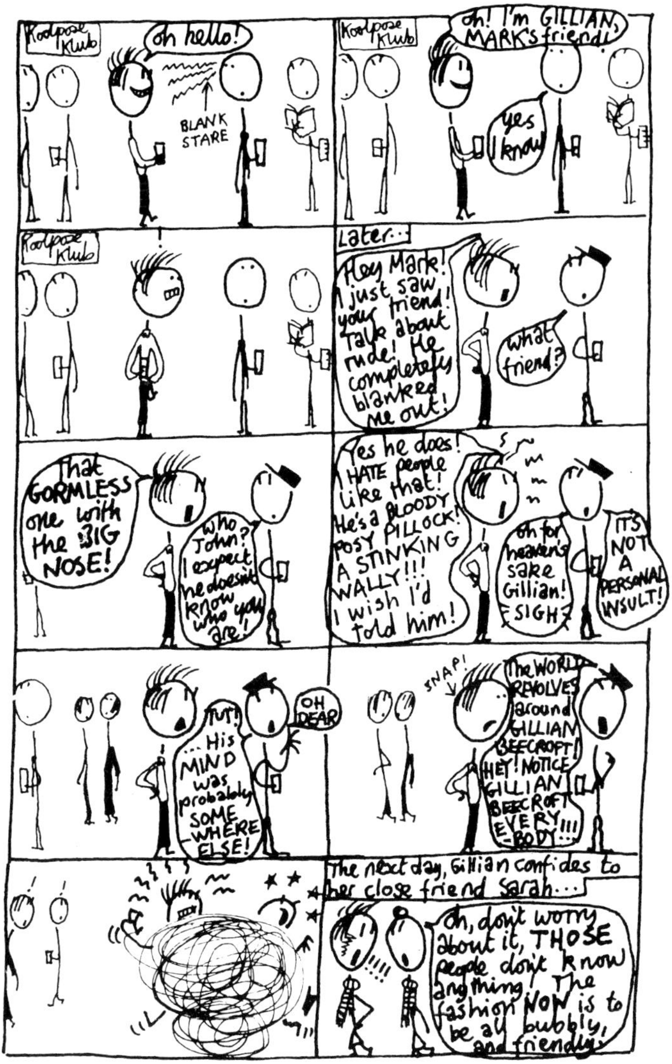
Koolpose Klub
oh hello!
BLANK STARE
Koolpose Klub
oh! I'm GILLIAN, MARK's friend!
yes I know
Koolpose Klub
!
Later...
Hey Mark! I just saw your friend! Talk about rude! He completely blanked me out!
what friend?
That GORMLESS one with the BIG NOSE!
Who John? I expect he doesn't know who you are!
Yes he does! I HATE people like that! He's a BLOODY POSY PILLOCK! A STINKING WALLY!!! I wish I'd told him!
oh for heaven's sake Gillian! SIGH
IT'S NOT A PERSONAL INSULT!
TUT! ...His MIND was probably SOME WHERE ELSE!
OH DEAR
SNAP!
The WORLD REVOLVES around GILLIAN BEECROFT! HEY! NOTICE GILLIAN BEECROFT EVERY-BODY!!!
!
!
The next day, Gillian confides to her close friend Sarah...
!!!!
Oh, don't worry about it, THOSE people don't know anything. The fashion NOW is to be all bubbly, and friendly.

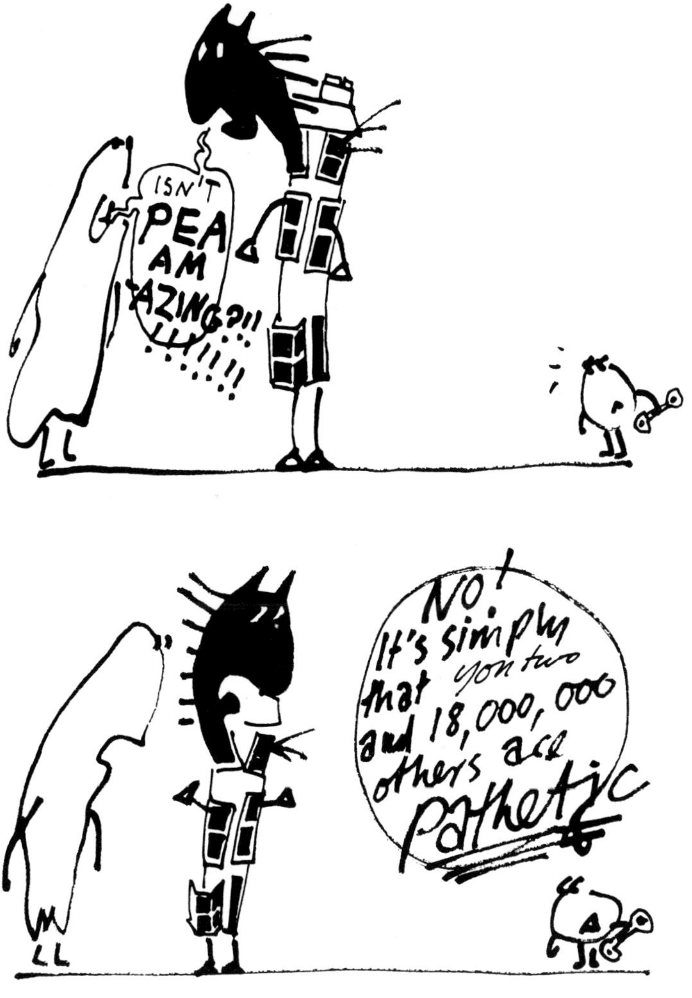
ISN'T PEA AM AZING?!!
No! It's simply that you two and 18,000,000 others are PATHETIC

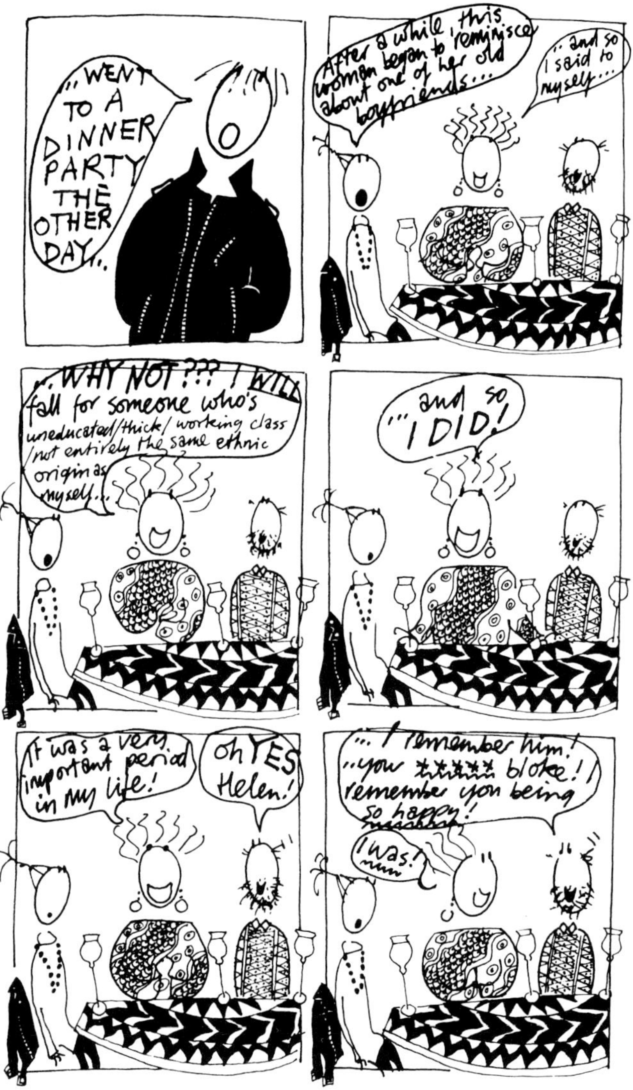
.. WENT TO A DINNER PARTY THE OTHER DAY..
After a while this woman began to 'reminisce' about one of her old boyfriends...
.. and so I said to myself...
.. WHY NOT??? I WILL fall for someone who's uneducated/thick/working class/not entirely the same ethnic origin as myself...
... and so, I DID!
It was a very important period in my life!
Oh YES Helen!
... I remember him! ..you ****** bloke! I remember you being so happy!
I was!

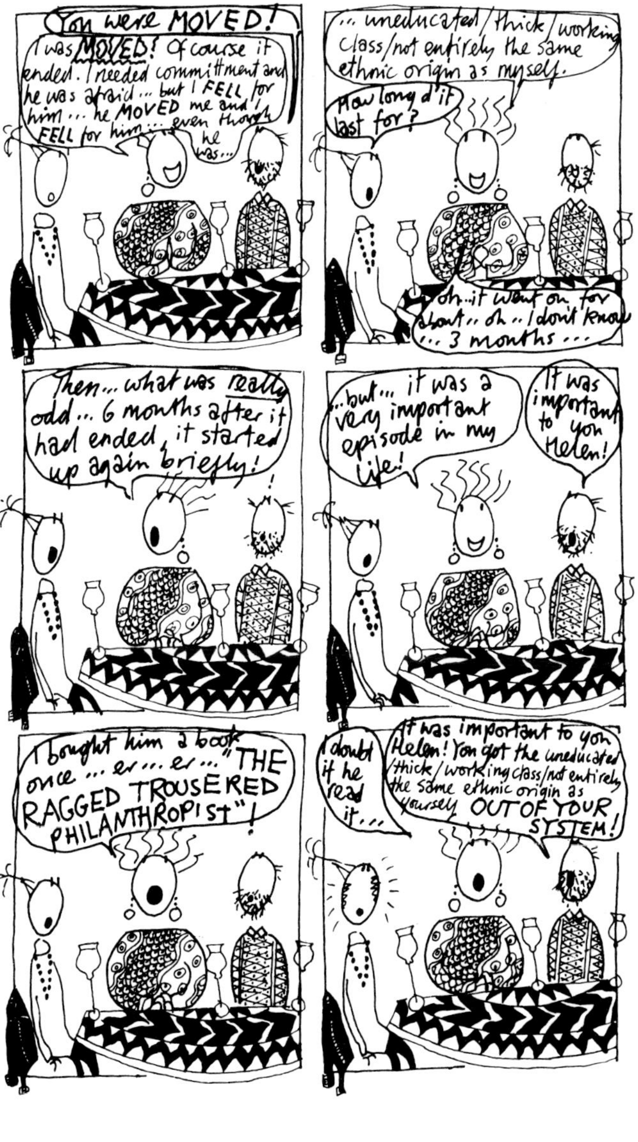
You were MOVED!
I was MOVED! Of course it ended. I needed committment and he was afraid... but I FELL for him... he MOVED me and I FELL for him... even though he was...
... uneducated/thick/working class/not entirely the same ethnic origin as myself.
How long d'it last for?
oh... it went on for about... oh... I don't know... 3 months...
Then... what was really odd... 6 months after it had ended, it started up again briefly!
...but... it was a very important episode in my life!
It was important to you Helen!
I bought him a book once... er... er... "THE RAGGED TROUSERED PHILANTHROPIST"!
I doubt if he read it...
It was important to you Helen! You got the uneducated/thick/working class/not entirely the same ethnic origin as yourself OUT OF YOUR SYSTEM!

Wet Lettuce Luck

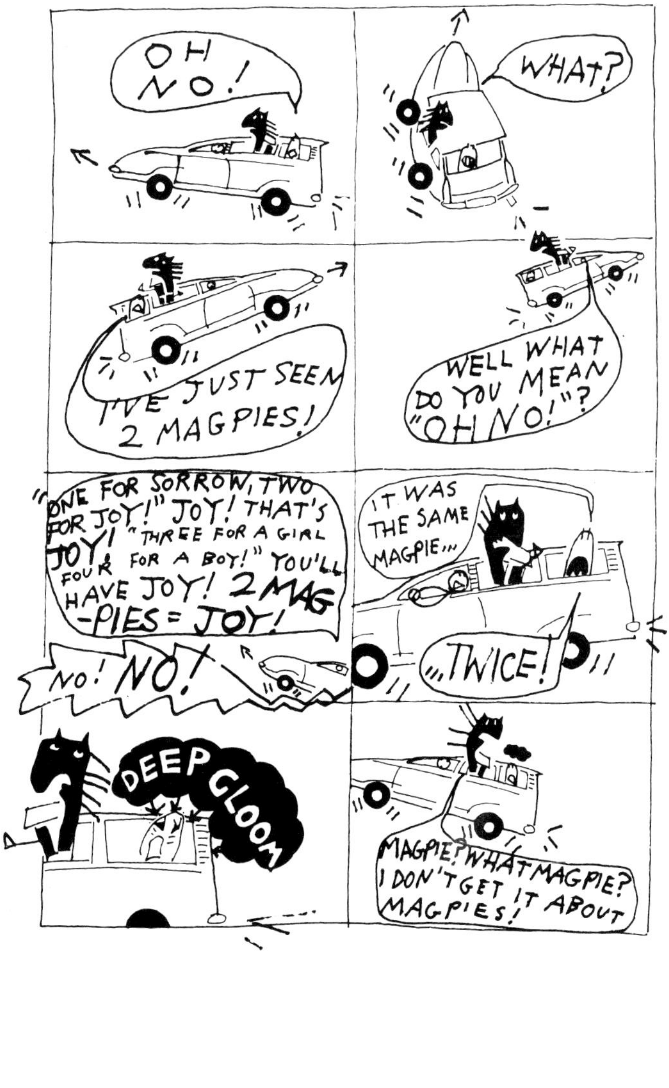
OH NO!
WHAT?
I'VE JUST SEEN 2 MAGPIES!
WELL WHAT DO YOU MEAN "OH NO!"?
"ONE FOR SORROW, TWO FOR JOY!" JOY! THAT'S JOY! "THREE FOR A GIRL & FOUR FOR A BOY!" YOU'LL HAVE JOY! 2 MAG-PIES = JOY!
IT WAS THE SAME MAGPIE...
NO! NO!
...TWICE!
DEEP GLOOM
MAGPIE? WHAT MAGPIE? I DON'T GET IT ABOUT MAGPIES!

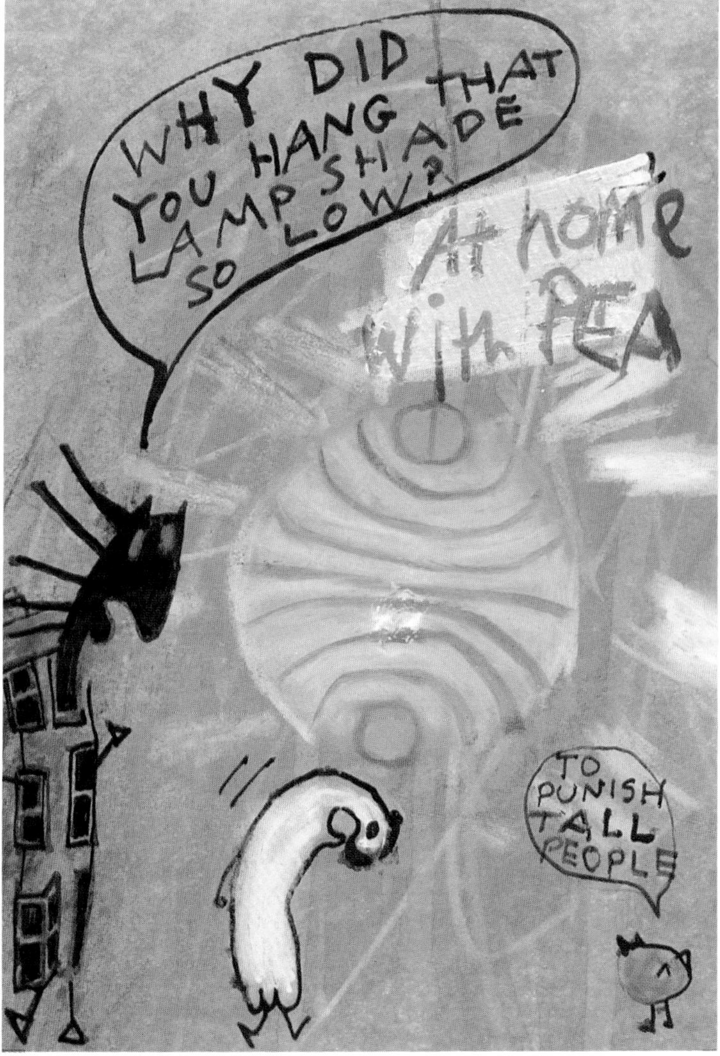
WHY DID YOU HANG THAT LAMPSHADE SO LOW?
At home with PEA
TO PUNISH TALL PEOPLE

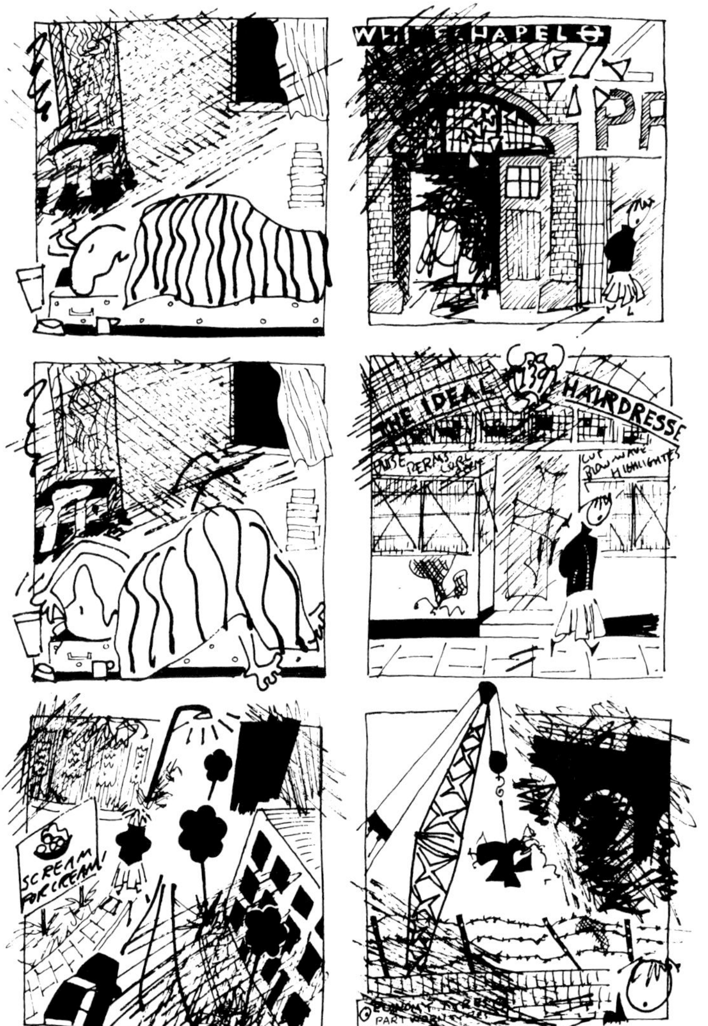
WHITECHAPEL
THE IDEAL
HAIRDRESSE
PERMS
CUT
HIGHLIGHTS
SCREAM FOR CREAM!
PART

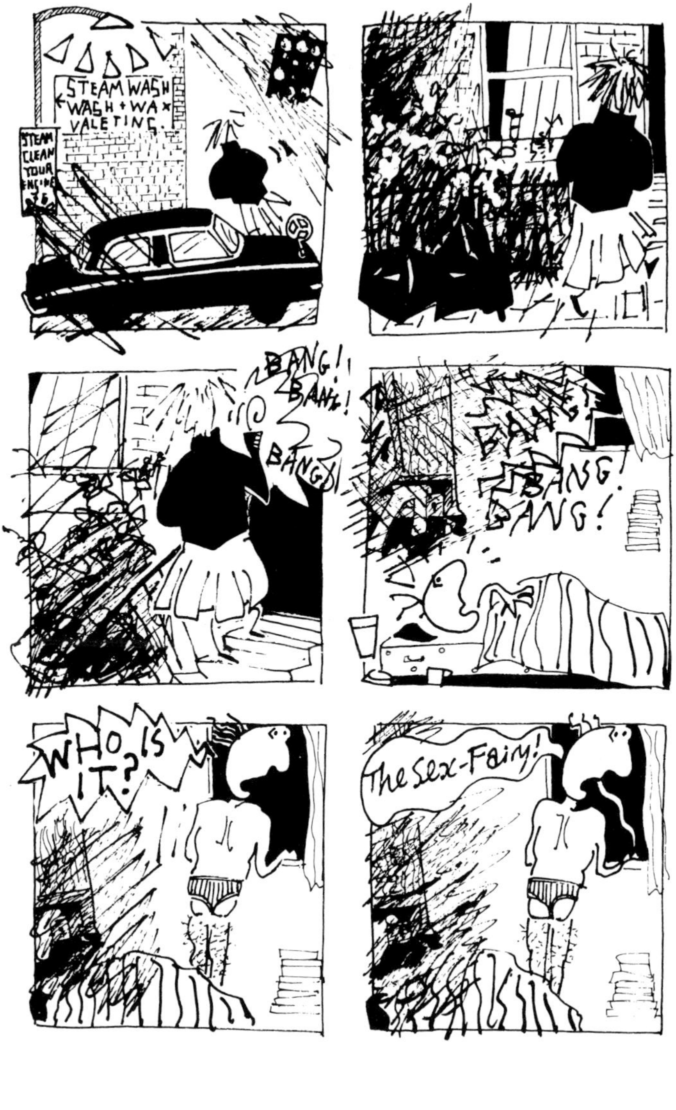

STEAM WASH
← WASH + WAX
VALETING.
STEAM CLEAN YOUR ENGINE
BANG!
BANG!
BANG!
BANG!
BANG!
BANG!
WHO IS IT?
The Sex-Fairy!

CAN YOU TAKE ON **PRE-FEMINIST MAN?** The management of PRE-FEMINIST MAN requires a lot of skill! A novice should not rush in blindly, and even an EXPERIENCED HAND should be prepared for a LONG SLOG UPHILL! RADICAL RE-STRUCTURING OF MIND-SETS is the name of the game when dealing with PRE-FEMINIST MAN ... and a point to remember ... PRE-FEMINIST MAN has had many years to become well entrenched in his attitudes and setbacks WILL OCCUR ... however ... patience and tenacity are often rewarded ... A RE-CONDITIONED GENTLEMAN of age 40+ can knock the spots off a callow toyboy who's never read a book in his life anyday!

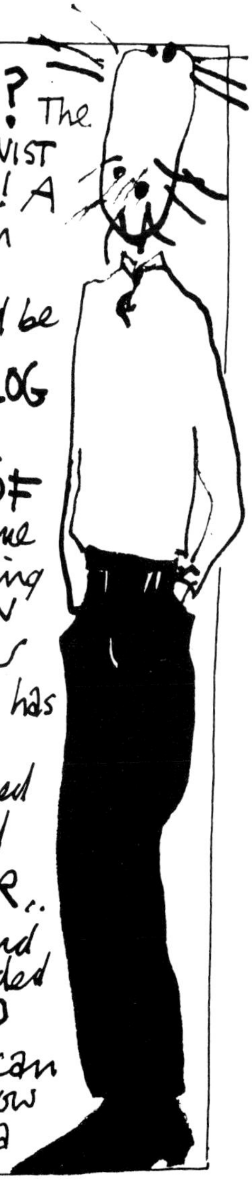

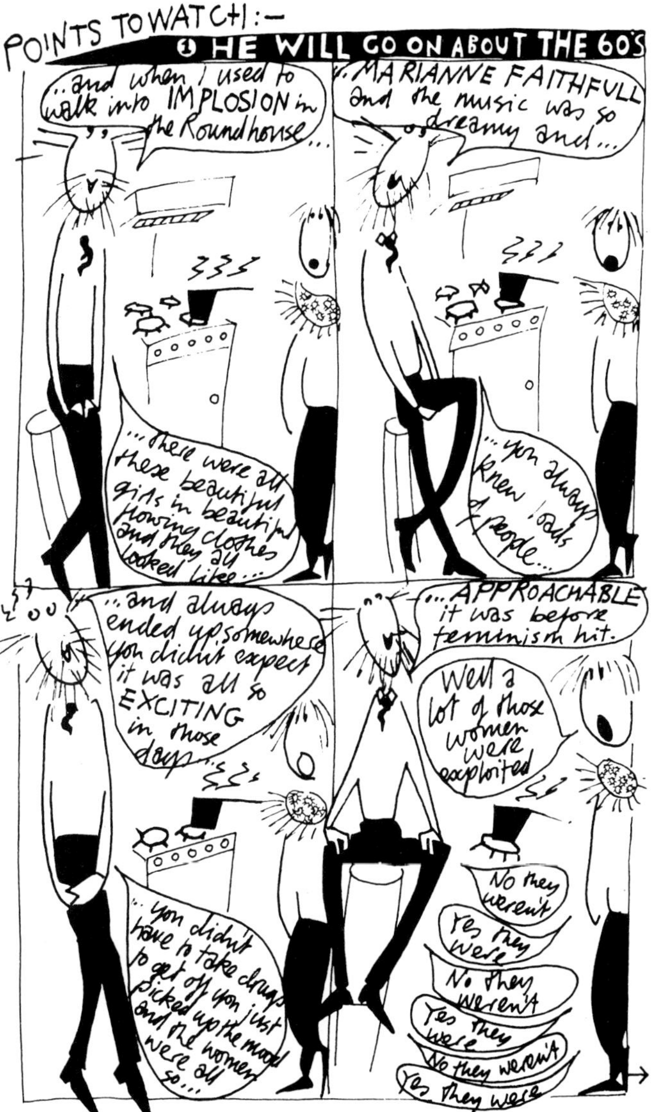
POINTS TO WATCH :-
1 HE WILL GO ON ABOUT THE 60'S
...and when I used to walk into IMPLOSION in the Roundhouse...
...there were all these beautiful girls in beautiful flowing clothes and they all looked like...
...MARIANNE FAITHFULL and the music was so dreamy and...
...you always knew loads of people...
...and always ended up somewhere you didn't expect it was all so EXCITING in those days...
...you didn't have to take drugs to get off you just picked up the mood and the women were all so...
...APPROACHABLE it was before feminism hit.
Well a lot of those women were exploited
No they weren't
Yes they were
No they weren't
Yes they were
No they weren't
Yes they were

2 HE WILL OBJECTIFY YOU

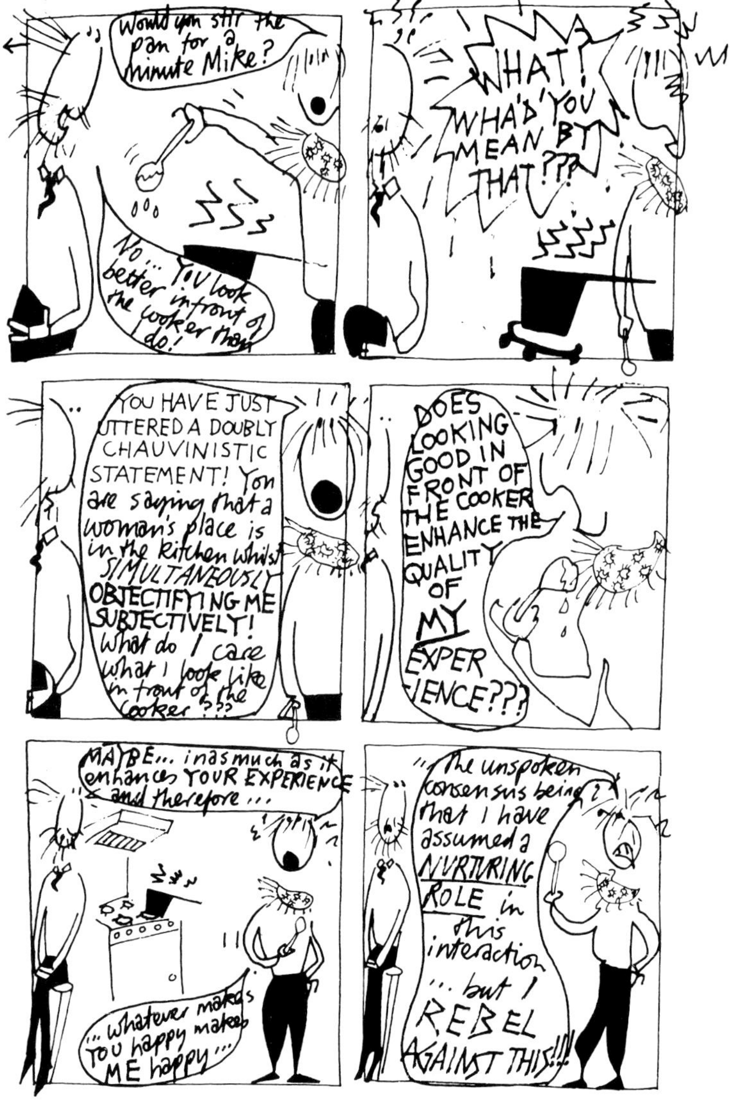
Would you stir the pan for a minute Mike?
No... You look better in front of the cooker than I do!
WHAT!
WHA'D YOU MEAN BY THAT???
YOU HAVE JUST UTTERED A DOUBLY CHAUVINISTIC STATEMENT! You are saying that a woman's place is in the kitchen whilst SIMULTANEOUSLY OBJECTIFYING ME SUBJECTIVELY! What do I care what I look like in front of the cooker???
DOES LOOKING GOOD IN FRONT OF THE COOKER ENHANCE THE QUALITY OF MY EXPERIENCE???
MAYBE... inasmuch as it enhances YOUR EXPERIENCE and therefore...
... whatever makes YOU happy makes ME happy...
The unspoken consensus being that I have assumed a NURTURING ROLE in this interaction
... but I REBEL AGAINST THIS!!!

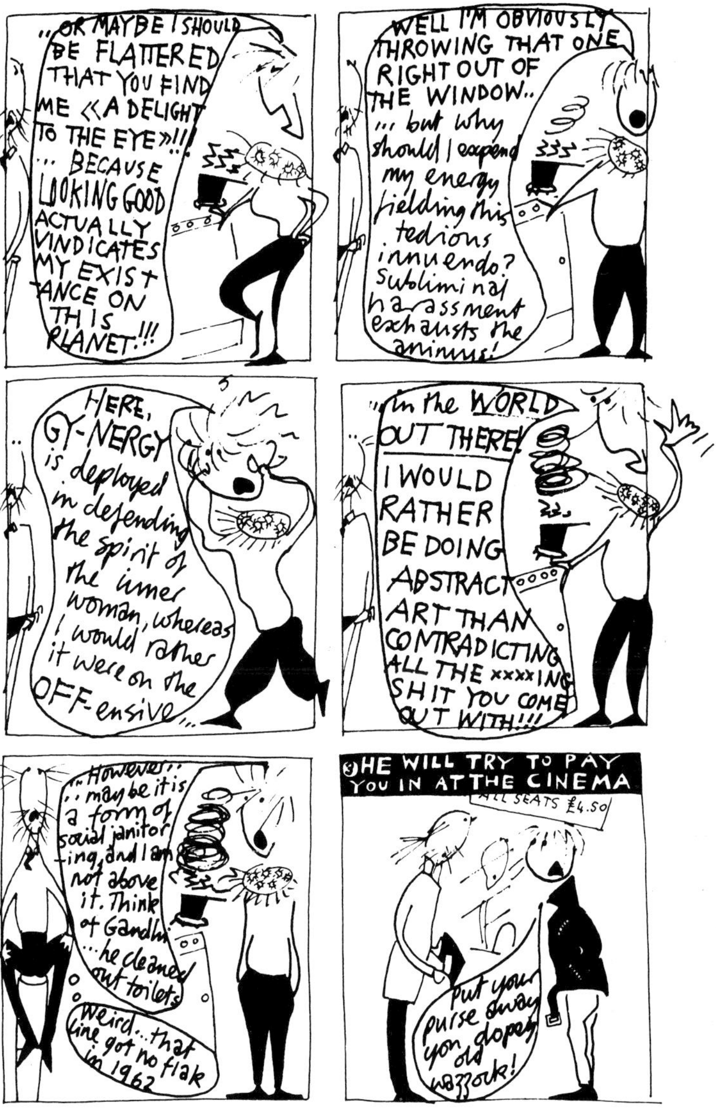
...OR MAYBE I SHOULD BE FLATTERED THAT YOU FIND ME «A DELIGHT TO THE EYE»!!! ... BECAUSE LOOKING GOOD ACTUALLY VINDICATES MY EXISTANCE ON THIS PLANET!!!
WELL I'M OBVIOUSLY THROWING THAT ONE RIGHT OUT OF THE WINDOW.. ... but why should I expend my energy fielding this tedious innuendo? Subliminal harassment exhausts the animus!
HERE, GY-NERGY is deployed in defending the spirit of the inner woman, whereas I would rather it were on the OFF-ensive...
...in the WORLD OUT THERE! I WOULD RATHER BE DOING ABSTRACT ART THAN CONTRADICTING ALL THE xxxxING SHIT YOU COME OUT WITH!!!
...However... ...maybe it is a form of social janitor-ing, and I am not above it. Think of Gandhi ...he cleaned out toilets
Weird... that line got no flak in 1962
HE WILL TRY TO PAY YOU IN AT THE CINEMA
ALL SEATS £4.50
Put your purse away yon dopey old wazzock!

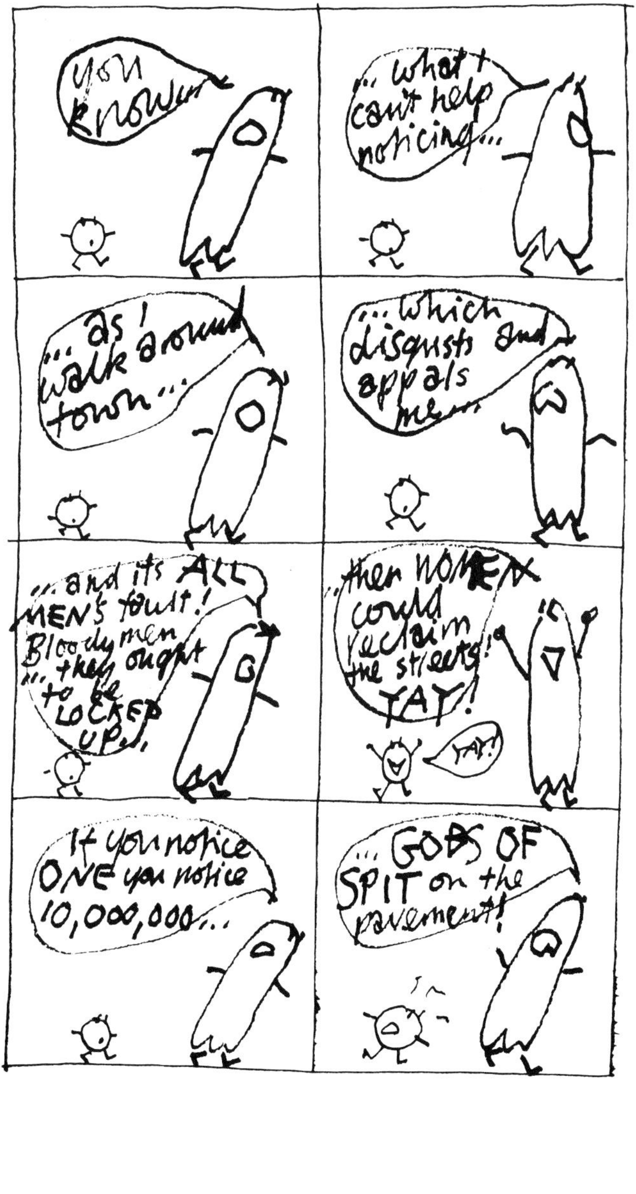
you know...
...what I can't help noticing...
...as I walk around town...
...which disgusts and appals me...
...and its ALL MEN'S fault! Bloody men they ought to be LOCKED UP...
...then WOMEN could reclaim the streets! YAY!
YAY!
If you notice ONE you notice 10,000,000...
...GOBS OF SPIT on the pavement!

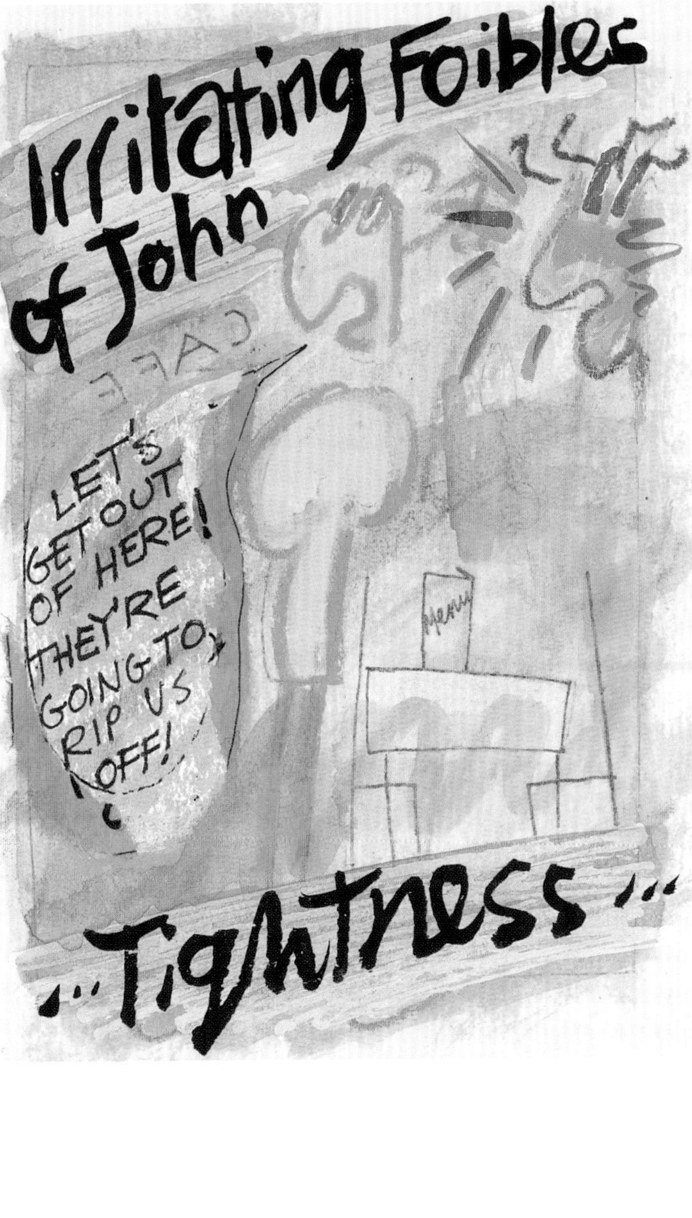
Irritating Foibles of John
CAFE
LET'S GET OUT OF HERE! THEY'RE GOING TO RIP US OFF!
Menu
..."Tightness"...

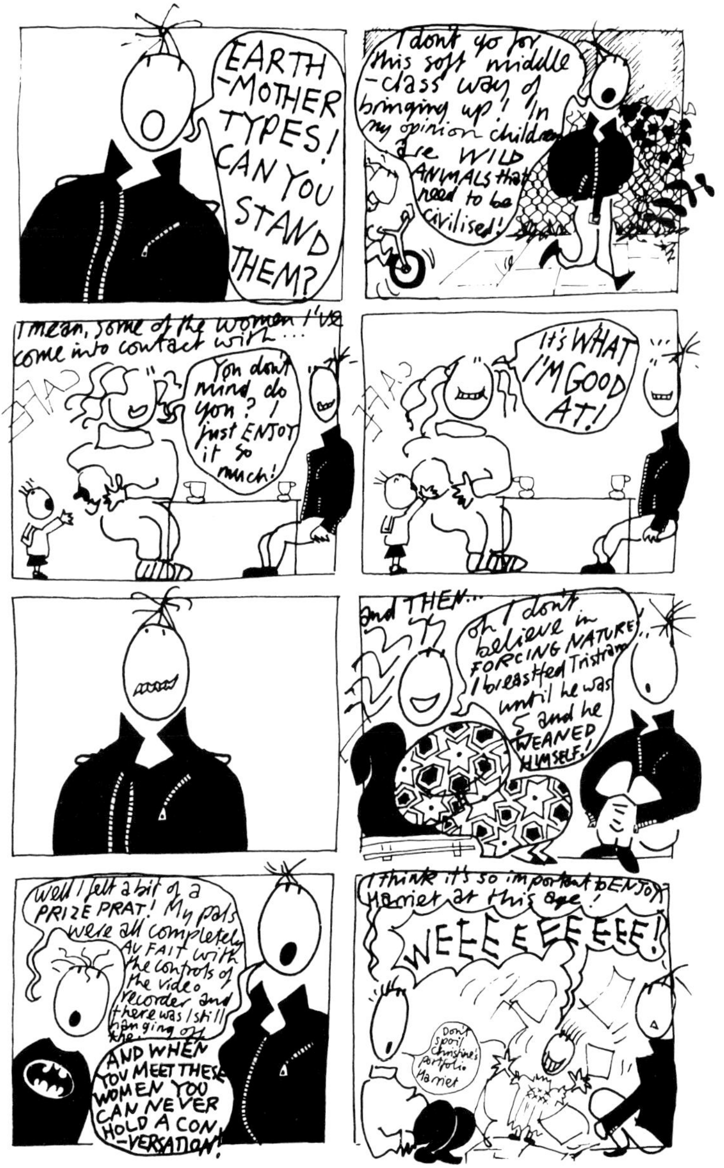
EARTH-MOTHER TYPES! CAN YOU STAND THEM?
I don't go for this soft middle-class way of bringing up! In my opinion children are WILD ANIMALS that need to be civilised!
I mean, some of the women I've come into contact with...
You don't mind, do you? I just ENJOY it so much!
It's WHAT I'M GOOD AT!
and THEN...
Oh I don't believe in FORCING NATURE! I breastfed Tristram until he was 5 and he WEANED HIMSELF!
Well I felt a bit of a PRIZE PRAT! My pals were all completely AU FAIT with the controls of the video recorder and there was I still hanging off the...
AND WHEN YOU MEET THESE WOMEN YOU CAN NEVER HOLD A CON-VERSATION!
I think it's so important to ENJOY Harriet at this age!
WEEEEEEEEE!
Don't spoil Christine's portfolio Harriet

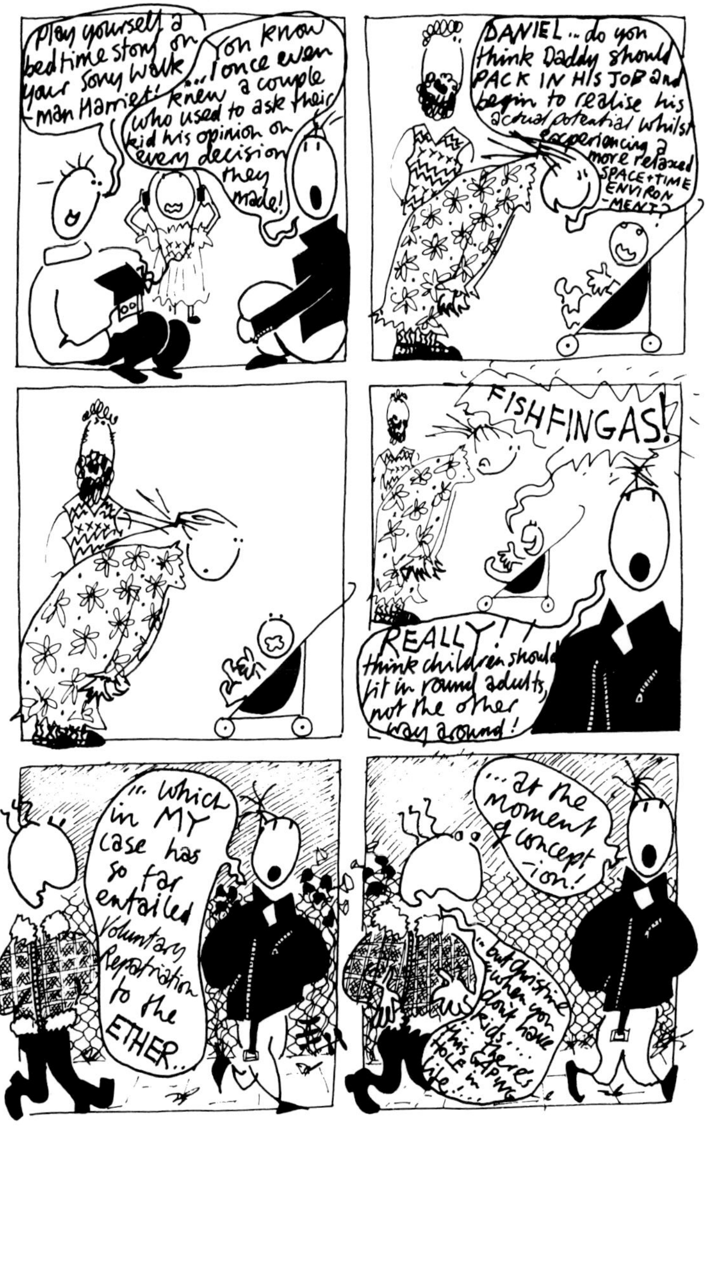
Play yourself a bedtime story on your Sony Walk-man Harriet!
You know ... I once even knew a couple who used to ask their kid his opinion on every decision they made!
DANIEL .. do you think Daddy should PACK IN HIS JOB and begin to realise his actual potential whilst experiencing a more relaxed SPACE+TIME ENVIRON-MENT?
FISHFINGAS!
REALLY!! think children should fit in round adults, not the other way around!
.. which in MY case has so far entailed Voluntary Repatriation to the ETHER..
... at the moment of concept-ion!
.. but Christine when you don't have kids... there's this GAPING HOLE in life...!

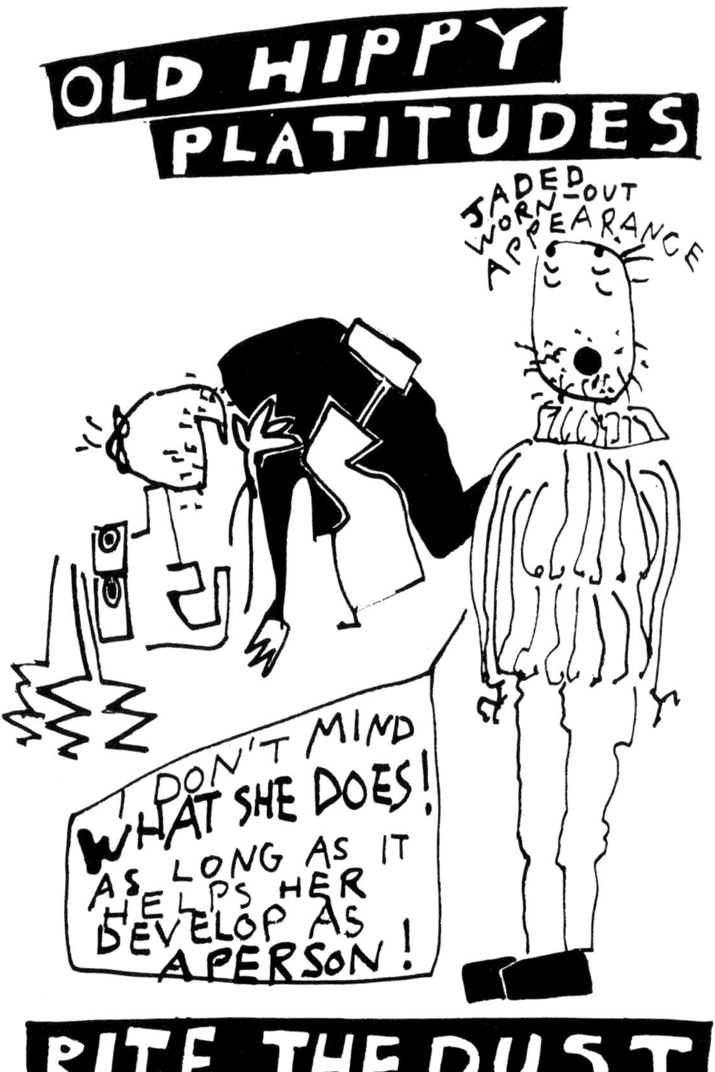
OLD HIPPY PLATITUDES
JADED WORN-OUT APPEARANCE
I DON'T MIND WHAT SHE DOES! AS LONG AS IT HELPS HER DEVELOP AS A PERSON!
BITE THE DUST

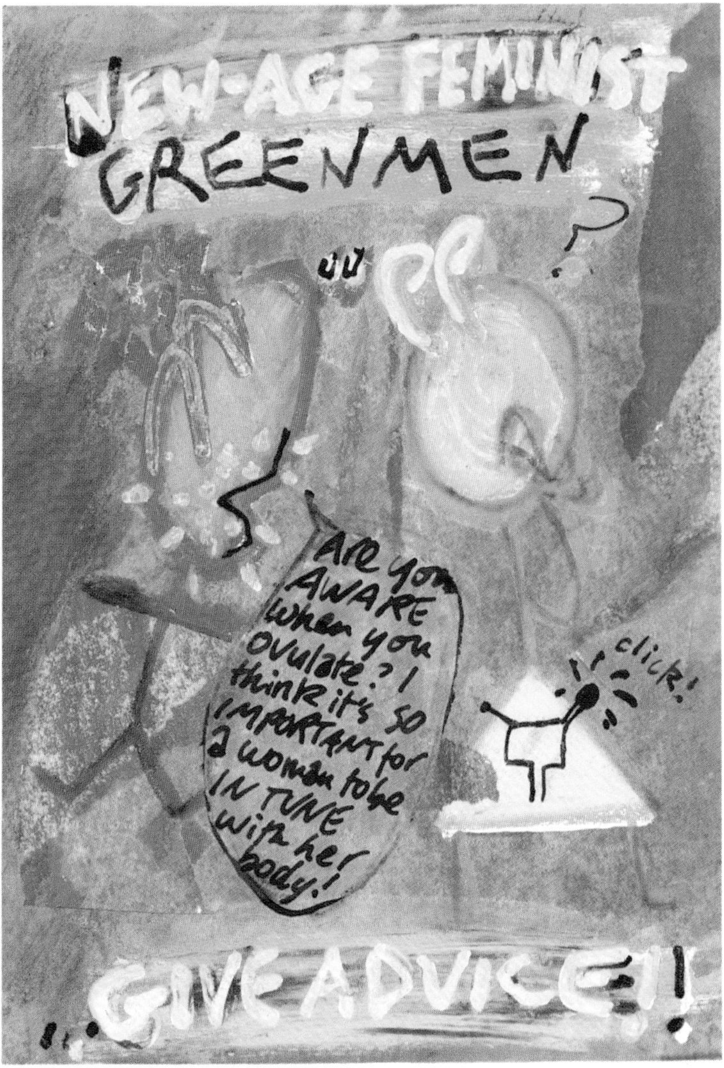
NEW-AGE FEMINIST GREENMEN
Are you AWARE when you ovulate? I think it's so IMPORTANT for a woman to be IN TUNE with her body!
click!
..GIVE ADVICE!

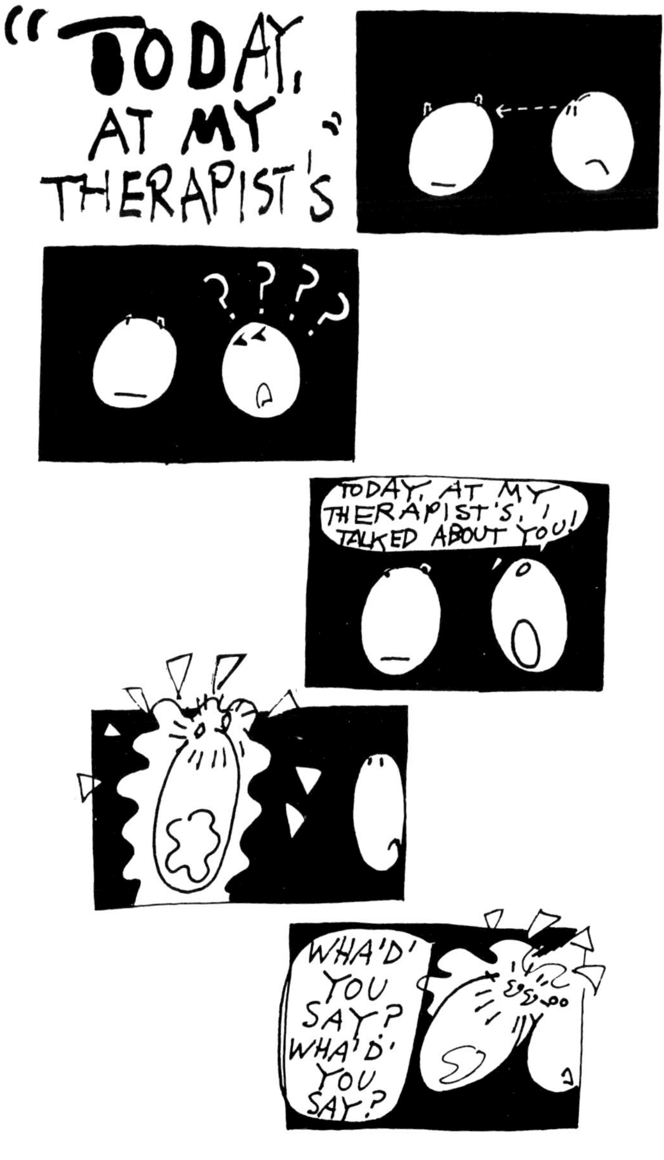
"TODAY, AT MY THERAPIST'S"
TODAY, AT MY THERAPIST'S, I TALKED ABOUT YOU!
WHA'D' YOU SAY? WHA'D' YOU SAY?

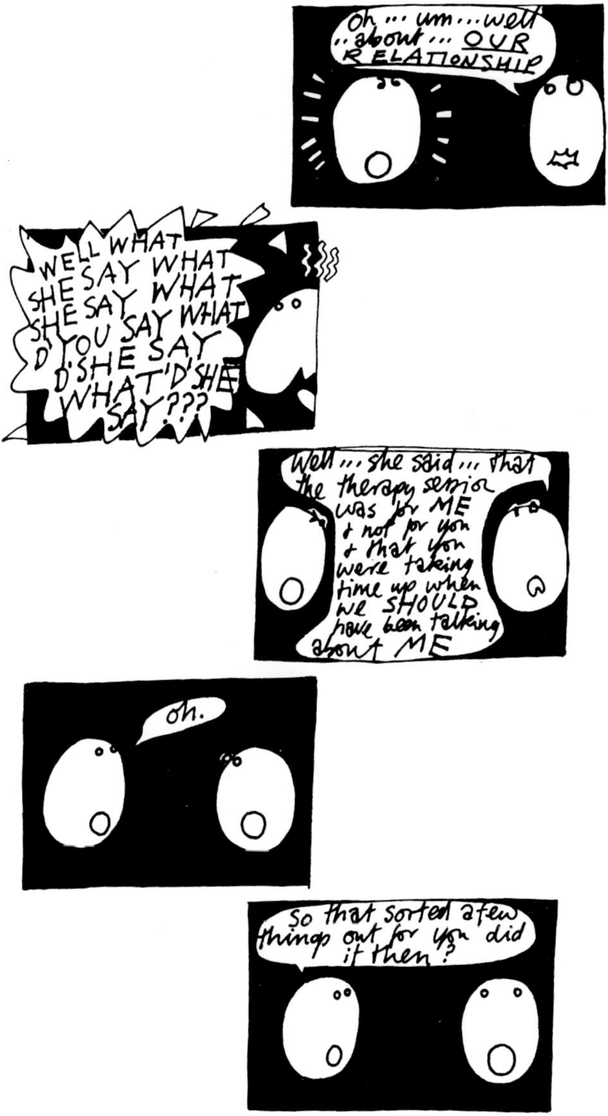
oh ... um ... well ... about ... OUR RELATIONSHIP
WELL WHAT SHE SAY WHAT SHE SAY WHAT SHE SAY WHAT D'YOU SAY WHAT D'SHE SAY D'SHE WHAT'D'SHE WHAT D'SHE SAY???
Well ... she said ... that the therapy session was for ME & not for you & that you were taking time up when we SHOULD have been talking about ME
oh.
So that sorted a few things out for you did it then?

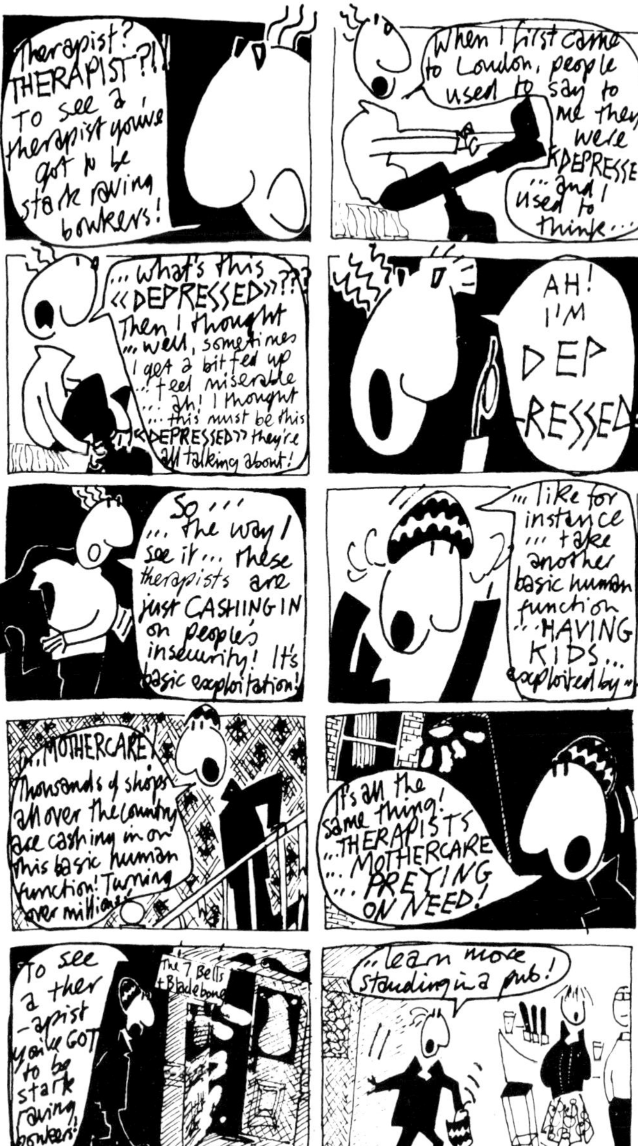

Therapist? THERAPIST?! To see a therapist you've got to be stark raving bonkers!
When I first came to London, people used to say to me they were «DEPRESSED» ... and I used to think...
... what's this «DEPRESSED»??? Then I thought ... well, sometimes I get a bit fed up ... feel miserable ... ah! I thought ... this must be this «DEPRESSED» they're all talking about!
AH! I'M DEP-RESSED!
So ... the way I see it ... these therapists are just CASHING IN on people's insecurity! It's basic exploitation!
... like for instance ... take another basic human function ... HAVING KIDS ... exploited by ...
... MOTHERCARE! Thousands of shops all over the country are cashing in on this basic human function! Turning over millions!
It's all the same thing! THERAPISTS ... MOTHERCARE ... PREYING ON NEED!
To see a ther-apist you've GOT to be stark raving bonkers!
The 7 Bells + Bladebone
... learn more standing in a pub!

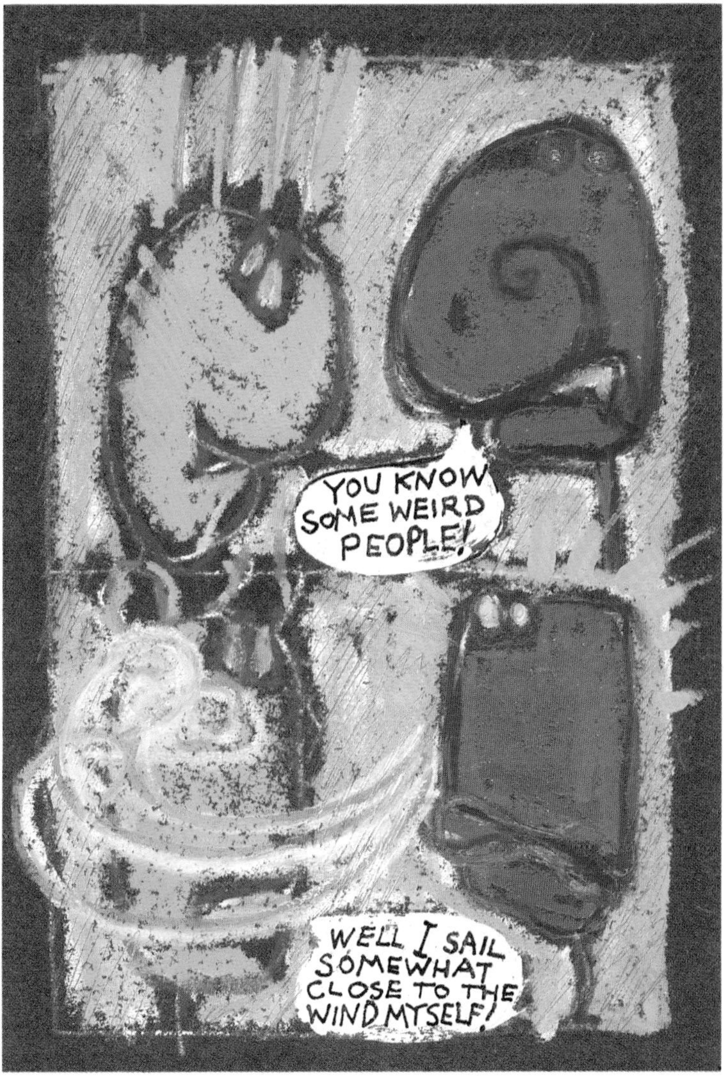
YOU KNOW SOME WEIRD PEOPLE!
WELL I SAIL SOMEWHAT CLOSE TO THE WIND MYSELF!

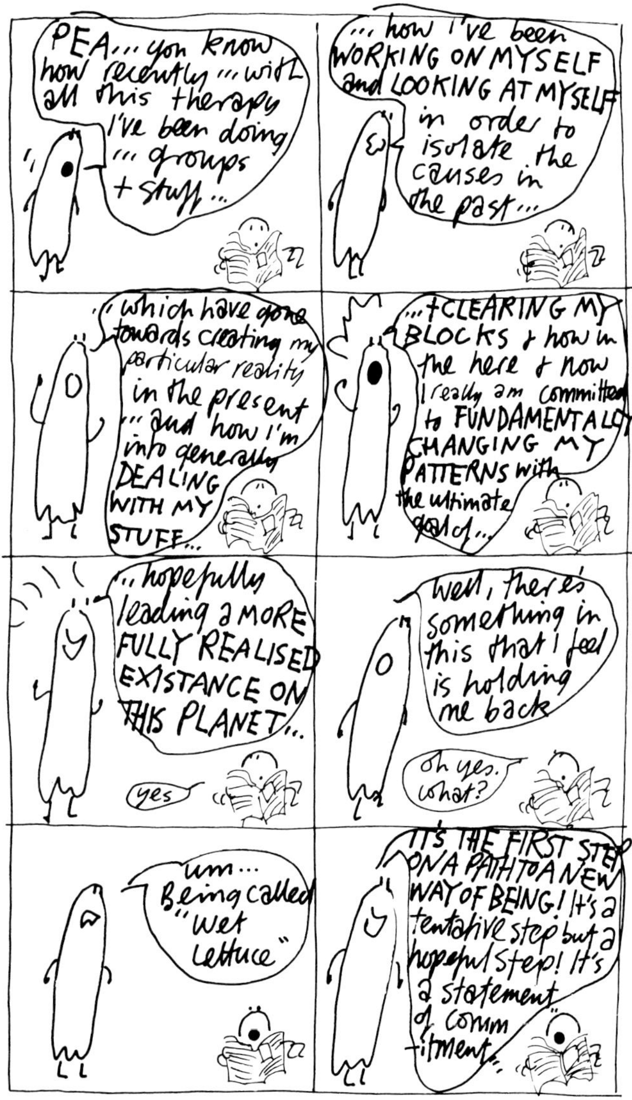
PEA... you know how recently ... with all this therapy I've been doing ... groups + stuff...
... how I've been WORKING ON MYSELF and LOOKING AT MYSELF in order to isolate the causes in the past...
... which have gone towards creating my particular reality in the present ... and how I'm into generally DEALING WITH MY STUFF...
... + CLEARING MY BLOCKS + how in the here + now I really am committed to FUNDAMENTALLY CHANGING MY PATTERNS with the ultimate goal of...
... hopefully leading a MORE FULLY REALISED EXISTANCE ON THIS PLANET...
yes
Well, there's something in this that I feel is holding me back
oh yes. what?
um... Being called "wet lettuce"
IT'S THE FIRST STEP ON A PATH TO A NEW WAY OF BEING! It's a tentative step but a hopeful step! It's a statement of comm-itment...

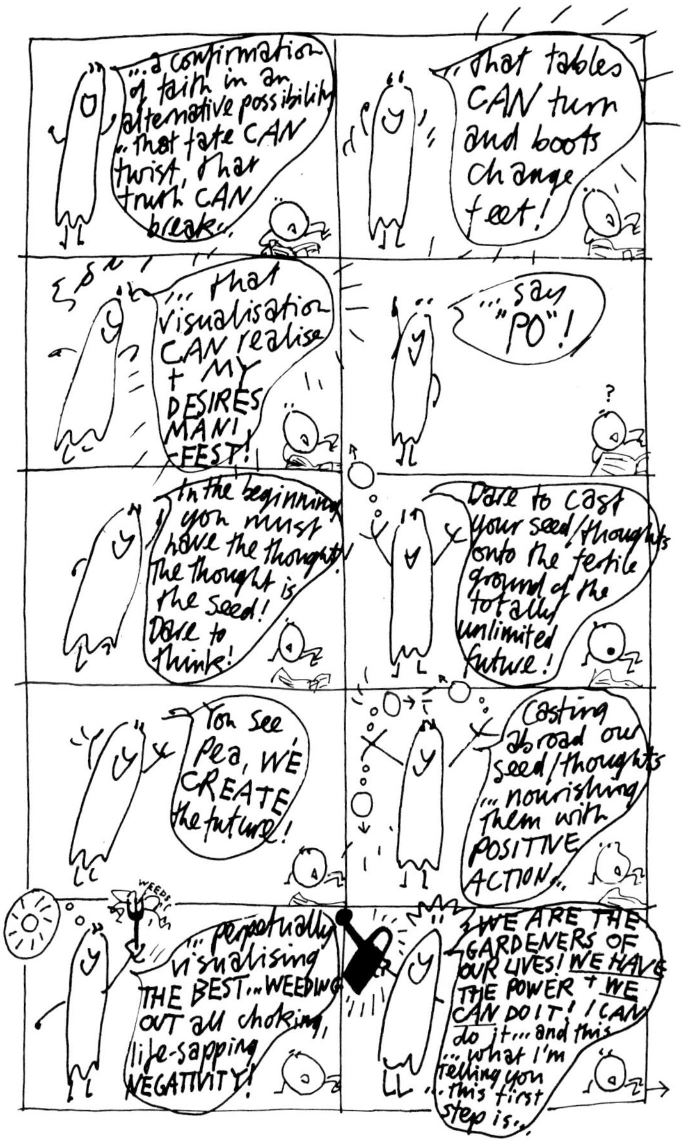
...a confirmation of faith in an alternative possibility ...that fate CAN twist, that truth CAN break...
...that tables CAN turn and boots change feet!
...that visualisation CAN realise + MY DESIRES MANI-FEST!
..."PO"! say
In the beginning you must have the thought. The thought is the seed! Dare to think!
Dare to cast your seed/thoughts onto the fertile ground of the totally unlimited future!
You see Pea, WE CREATE the future!
Casting abroad our seed/thoughts ...nourishing them with POSITIVE ACTION...
WEEDS
...perpetually visualising THE BEST...WEEDING OUT all choking, life-sapping NEGATIVITY!
WE ARE THE GARDENERS OF OUR LIVES! WE HAVE THE POWER + WE CAN DO IT! I CAN do it... and this ...what I'm telling you this first step is...

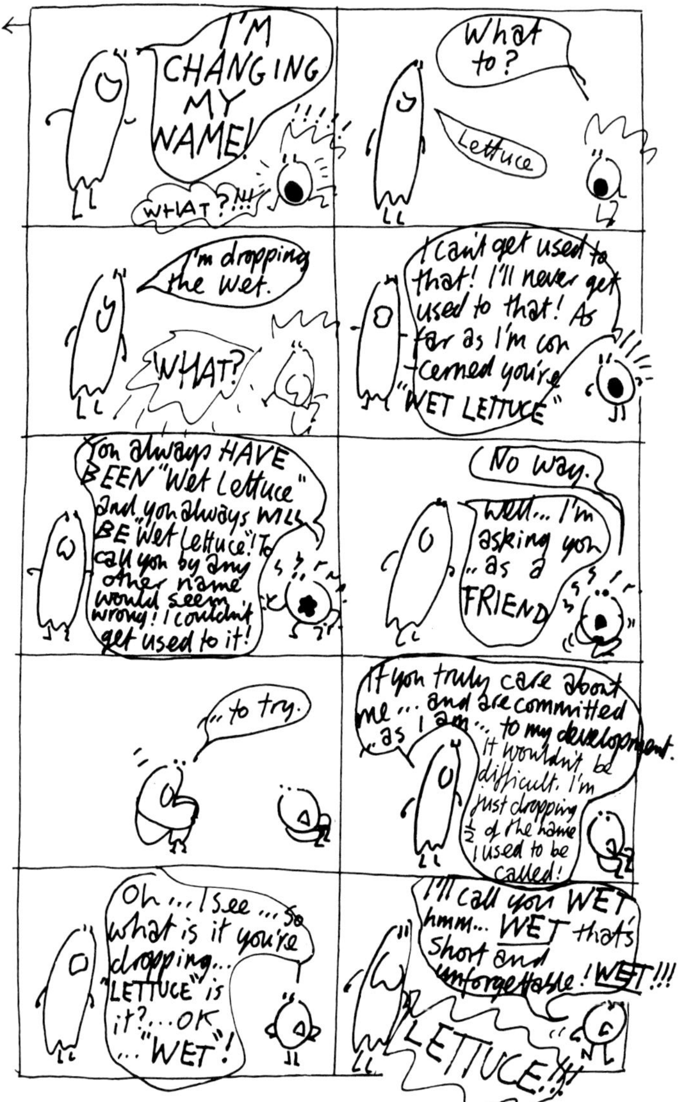
I'M CHANGING MY NAME!
WHAT?!!!
What to?
Lettuce
I'm dropping the Wet.
WHAT?
I can't get used to that! I'll never get used to that! As far as I'm concerned you're "WET LETTUCE"
You always HAVE BEEN "Wet Lettuce" and you always WILL BE Wet Lettuce! To call you by any other name would seem wrong! I couldn't get used to it!
No way.
Well... I'm asking you .. as a FRIEND
.. to try.
If you truly care about me ... and are committed .. as I am .. to my development. It wouldn't be difficult. I'm just dropping ½ of the name I used to be called!
Oh ... I see ... so what is it you're dropping... "LETTUCE" is it?... OK ... "WET"!
I'll call you WET hmm... WET that's short and unforgettable! WET!!!
LETTUCE!!!

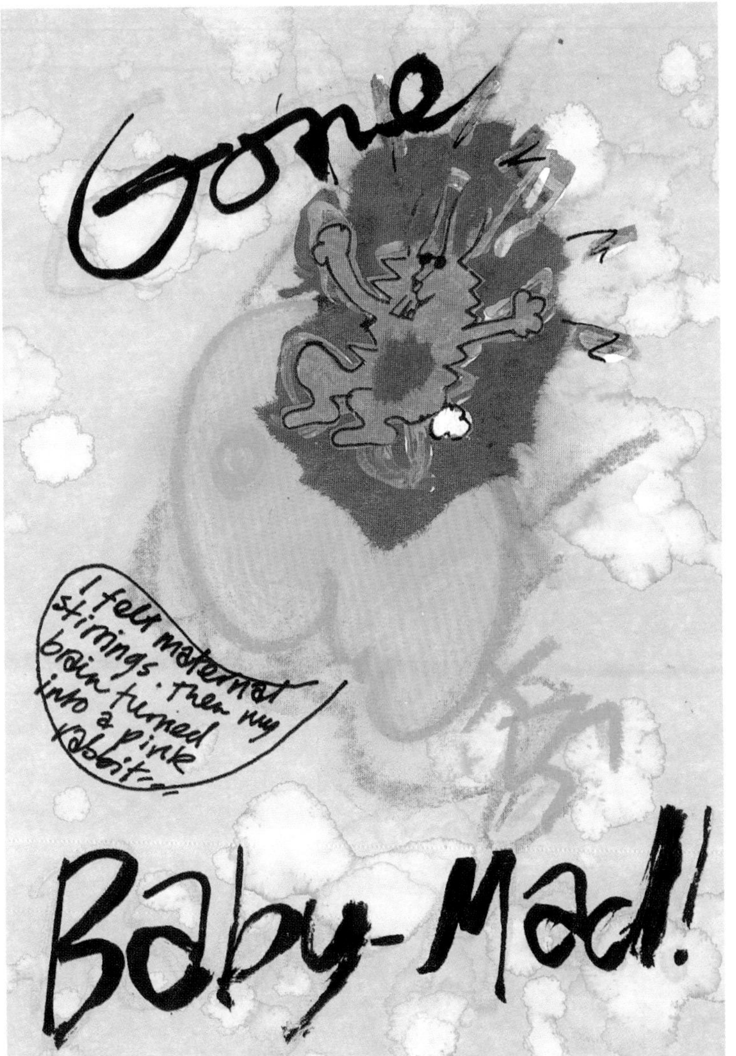
Gone
I felt maternal stirrings. Then my brain turned into a pink rabbit.
Baby-Mad!

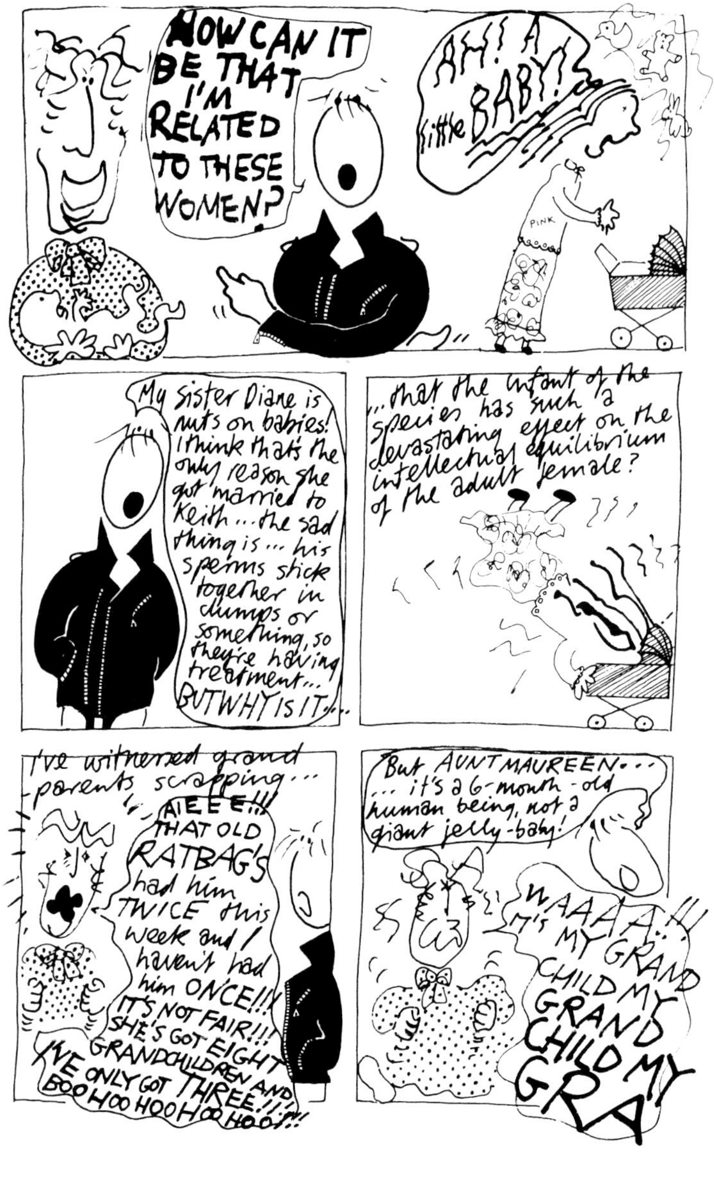
HOW CAN IT BE THAT I'M RELATED TO THESE WOMEN?
AH! A little BABY!
PINK
My sister Diane is nuts on babies! I think that's the only reason she got married to Keith... the sad thing is... his sperms stick together in clumps or something, so they're having treatment... BUT WHY IS IT...
...that the infant of the species has such a devastating effect on the intellectual equilibrium of the adult female?
I've witnessed grand-parents scrapping...
AIEEE!!! THAT OLD RATBAG'S had him TWICE this week and I haven't had him ONCE!!! IT'S NOT FAIR!!! SHE'S GOT EIGHT GRANDCHILDREN AND I'VE ONLY GOT THREE!!! BOO HOO HOO HOO HOO!!!
But AUNT MAUREEN... ...it's a 6-month-old human being, not a giant jelly-baby!
WAAAA!!! IT'S MY GRANDCHILD MY GRANDCHILD MY GRA

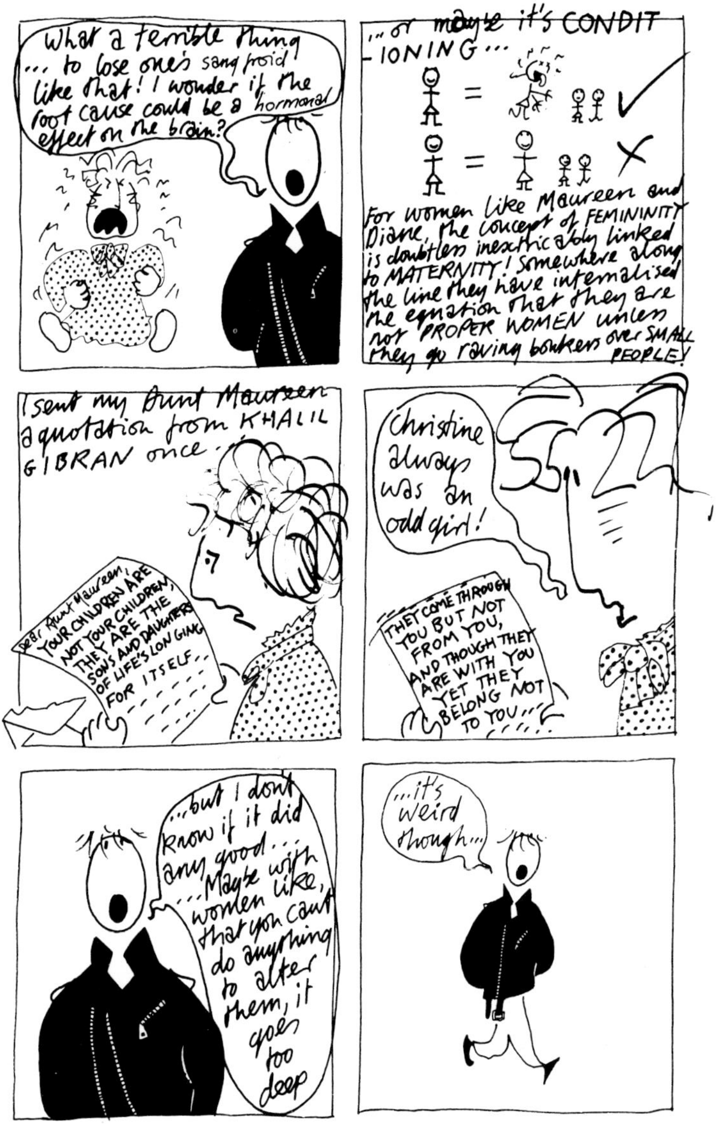
What a terrible thing ... to lose one's sang froid like that! I wonder if the root cause could be a hormonal effect on the brain?
...or maybe it's CONDIT-IONING...
For women like Maureen and Diane, the concept of FEMININITY is doubtless inextricably linked to MATERNITY! Somewhere along the line they have internalised the equation that they are not PROPER WOMEN unless they go raving bonkers over SMALL PEOPLE!
I sent my Aunt Maureen a quotation from KHALIL GIBRAN once...
Dear Aunt Maureen, YOUR CHILDREN ARE NOT YOUR CHILDREN, THEY ARE THE SONS AND DAUGHTERS OF LIFE'S LONGING FOR ITSELF.
Christine always was an odd girl!
THEY COME THROUGH YOU BUT NOT FROM YOU, AND THOUGH THEY ARE WITH YOU YET THEY BELONG NOT TO YOU...
...but I don't know if it did any good... Maybe with women like that you can't do anything to alter them, it goes too deep
...it's weird though...

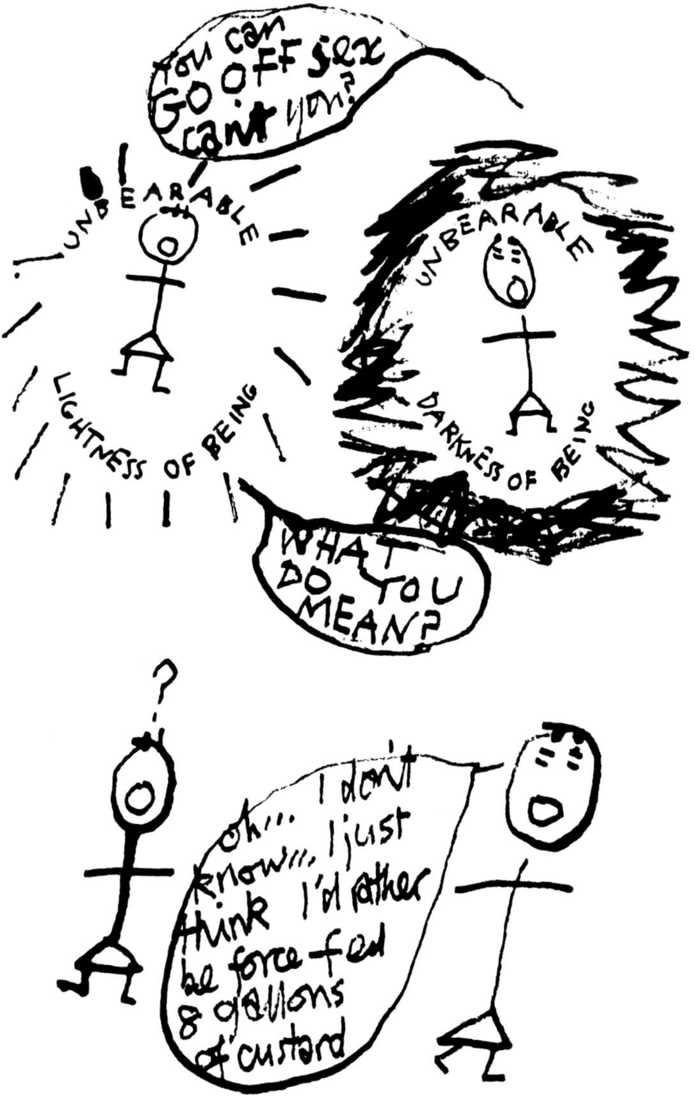
You can GO OFF sex can't you?
UNBEARABLE LIGHTNESS OF BEING
UNBEARABLE DARKNESS OF BEING
WHAT DO YOU MEAN?
?
oh... I don't know... I just think I'd rather be force-fed 8 gallons of custard

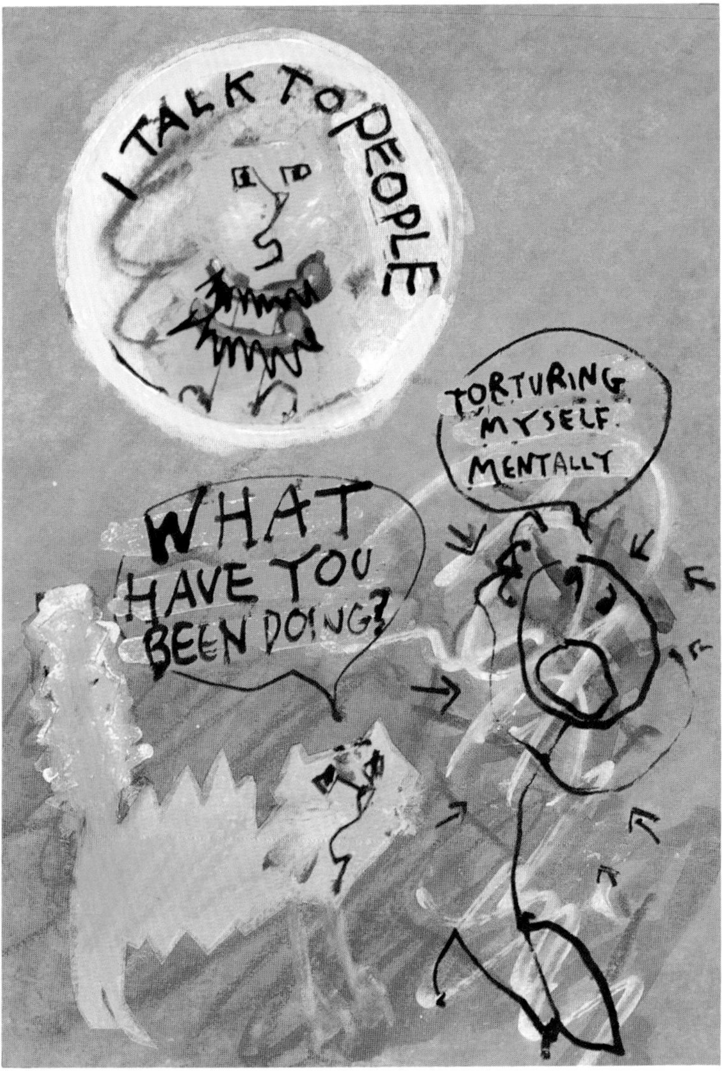
I TALK TO PEOPLE
TORTURING MYSELF MENTALLY
WHAT HAVE YOU BEEN DOING?

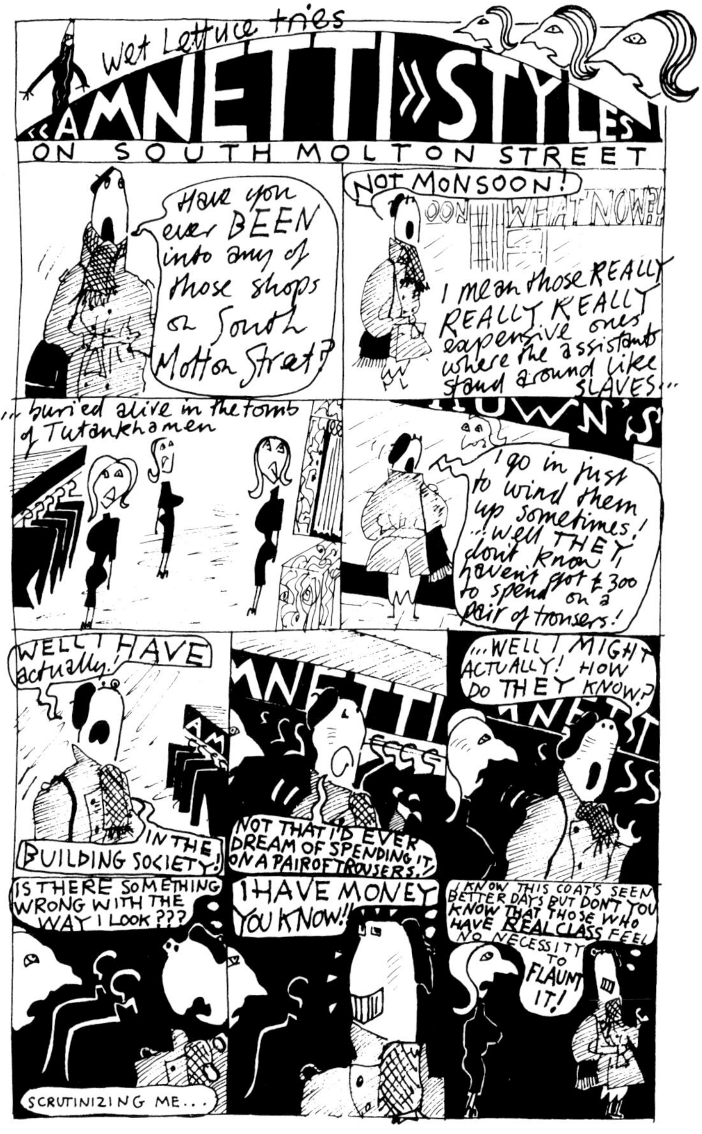
Wet Lettuce tries
«AMNETTI» STYLES
ON SOUTH MOLTON STREET
Have you ever BEEN into any of those shops on South Molton Street?
NOT MONSOON!
I mean those REALLY REALLY REALLY expensive ones where the assistants stand around like SLAVES...
...buried alive in the tomb of Tutankhamen
I go in just to wind them up sometimes! ...well THEY don't know I haven't got £300 to spend on a pair of trousers!
WELL I HAVE actually!
IN THE BUILDING SOCIETY!
NOT THAT I'D EVER DREAM OF SPENDING IT ON A PAIR OF TROUSERS.
...WELL I MIGHT ACTUALLY! HOW DO THEY KNOW?
IS THERE SOMETHING WRONG WITH THE WAY I LOOK???
SCRUTINIZING ME...
I HAVE MONEY YOU KNOW!
I KNOW THIS COAT'S SEEN BETTER DAYS BUT DON'T YOU KNOW THAT THOSE WHO HAVE REAL CLASS FEEL NO NECESSITY TO FLAUNT IT!

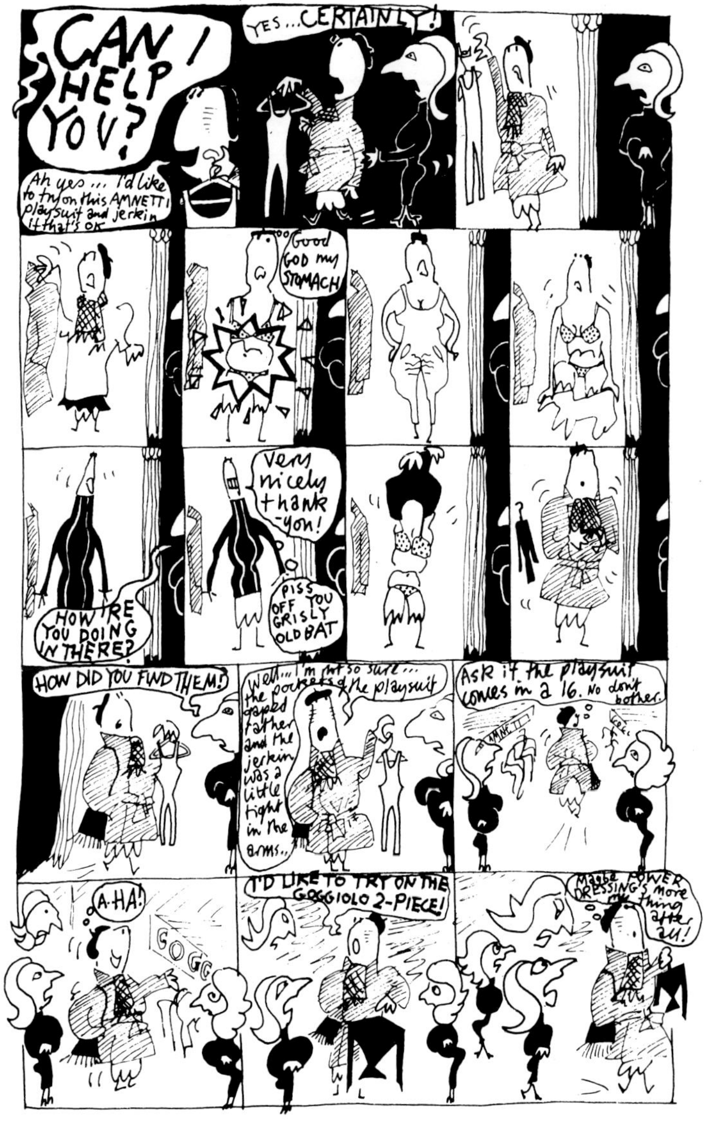
CAN I HELP YOU?
Ah yes ... I'd like to try on this AMNETTI playsuit and jerkin if that's OK
YES...CERTAINLY!
Good GOD my STOMACH
HOW'RE YOU DOING IN THERE?
Very nicely thank-you!
PISS OFF YOU GRISLY OLD BAT
HOW DID YOU FIND THEM?
Well... I'm not so sure... the pockets of the playsuit gaped rather and the jerkin was a little tight in the arms..
Ask if the playsuit comes in a 16. No don't bother.
AMNETTI
A-HA!
GOGG
I'D LIKE TO TRY ON THE GOGGIOLO 2-PIECE!
Maybe POWER DRESSING's more my thing after all!

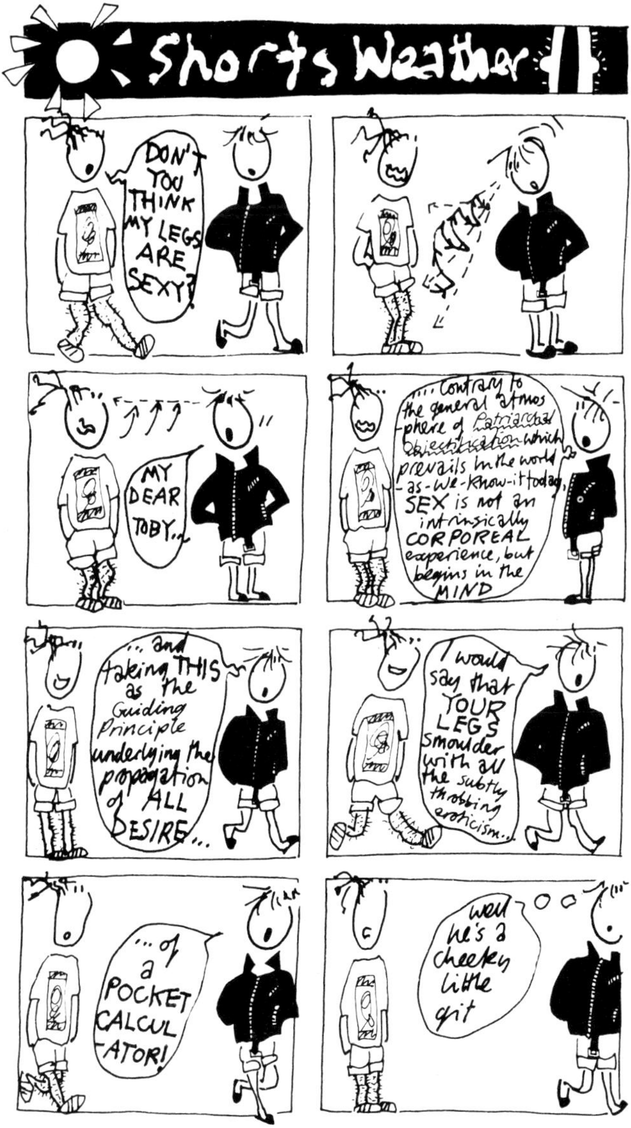
Shorts Weather
DON'T YOU THINK MY LEGS ARE SEXY?
MY DEAR TOBY...
....Contrary to the general atmos-phere of Patriarchal Objectification which prevails in the world-as-we-know-it today, SEX is not an intrinsically CORPOREAL experience, but begins in the MIND
... and taking THIS as the Guiding Principle underlying the propagation of ALL DESIRE...
I would say that YOUR LEGS smoulder with all the subtly throbbing eroticism...
... of a POCKET CALCUL-ATOR!
well he's a cheeky little git

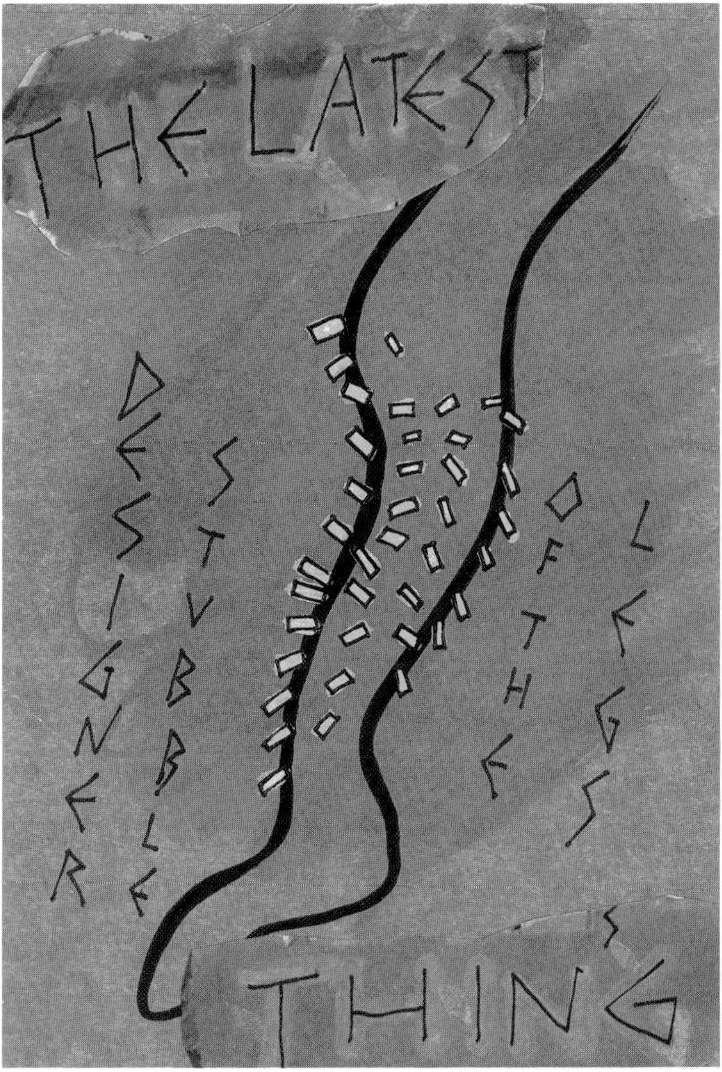
THE LATEST
DESIGNER
STUBBLE
OF THE
LEGS
THING

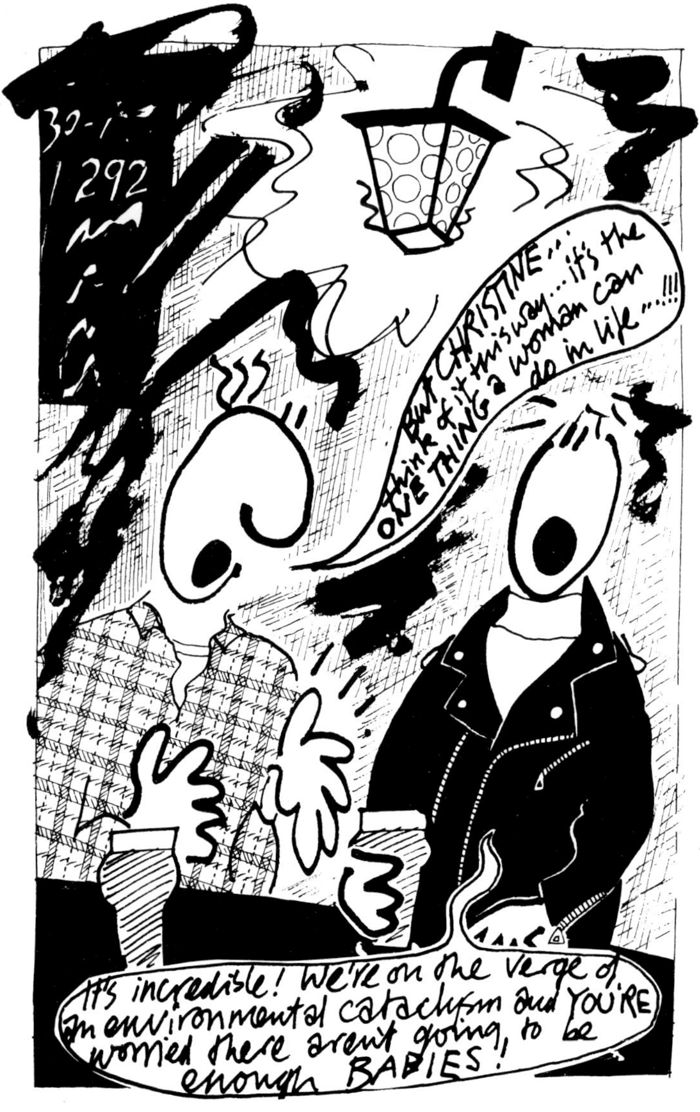

But CHRISTINE... think of it this way... it's the ONE THING a woman can do in life...!!!
It's incredible! We're on the verge of an environmental cataclysm and YOU'RE worried there aren't going to be enough BABIES!